W9-BUI-204

IMMERSION
Bible Studies

JAMES
1 & 2 PETER
1, 2 & 3 JOHN
JUDE

Praise for IMMERSION

"IMMERSION BIBLE STUDIES is a powerful tool in helping readers to hear God speak through Scripture and to experience a deeper faith as a result."
Adam Hamilton, author of *24 Hours That Changed the World*

"This unique Bible study makes Scripture come alive for students. Through the study, students are invited to move beyond the head into the heart of faith."
Bishop Joseph W. Walker, author of *Love and Intimacy*

"If you're looking for a deeper knowledge and understanding of God's Word, you must dive into IMMERSION BIBLE STUDIES. Whether in a group setting or as an individual, you will experience God and his unconditional love for each of us in a whole new way."
Pete Wilson, founding and senior pastor of Cross Point Church

"This beautiful series helps readers become fluent in the words and thoughts of God, for purposes of illumination, strength building, and developing a closer walk with the One who loves us so."
Laurie Beth Jones, author of *Jesus, CEO* and *The Path*

"The IMMERSION BIBLE STUDIES series is no less than a game changer. It ignites the purpose and power of Scripture by showing us how to do more than just know God or love God; it gives us the tools to love like God as well."
Shane Stanford, author of *You Can't Do Everything . . . So Do Something*

IMMERSION
Bible Studies

JAMES
1 & 2 PETER
1, 2 & 3 JOHN
JUDE

Michael E. Williams

Abingdon Press

Nashville

JAMES; 1 & 2 PETER; 1, 2 & 3 JOHN; JUDE
IMMERSION BIBLE STUDIES
by Michael E. Williams

Library of Congress Cataloging-in-Publication Data

Williams, Michael E. (Michael Edward), 1950–
  James 1–2, Peter 1,2,3, John, Jude : immersion Bible studies / Michael E. Williams.
    p. cm.
  ISBN 978-1-4267-0988-3 (curriculum—printed / text plus-cover : alk. paper) 1. Bible. N.T.
Catholic Epistles—Criticism, interpretation, etc. I. Title.
  BS2777.W455 2012
  227'.906—dc23

                                                                    2011050412

Editor: Jack A. Keller, Jr.
Leader Guide Writer: Martha Bettis Gee

12 13 14 15 16 17 18 19 20 21—10 9 8 7 6 5 4 3 2 1

Manufactured in the United States of America

Contents

Review Team

Diane Blum
Pastor
East End United Methodist Church
Nashville, Tennessee

Susan Cox
Pastor
McMurry United Methodist Church
Claycomo, Missouri

Margaret Ann Crain
Professor of Christian Education
Garrett-Evangelical Theological Seminary
Evanston, Illinois

Nan Duerling
Curriculum Writer and Editor
Cambridge, Maryland

Paul Escamilla
Pastor and Writer
St. John's United Methodist Church
Austin, Texas

James Hawkins
Pastor and Writer
Smyrna, Delaware

Andrew Johnson
Professor of New Testament
Nazarene Theological Seminary
Kansas City, Missouri

Snehlata Patel
Pastor
Woodrow United Methodist Church
Staten Island, New York

Emerson B. Powery
Professor of New Testament
Messiah College
Grantham, Pennsylvania

Clayton Smith
Pastoral Staff
Church of the Resurrection
Leawood, Kansas

Harold Washington
Professor of Hebrew Bible
Saint Paul School of Theology
Kansas City, Missouri

Carol Wehrheim
Curriculum Writer and Editor
Princeton, New Jersey

IMMERSION BIBLE STUDIES

A fresh new look at the Bible, from beginning to end,
and what it means in your life.

Welcome to IMMERSION!

We've asked some of the leading Bible scholars, teachers, and pastors to help us with a new kind of Bible study. IMMERSION remains true to Scripture but always asks, "Where are you in your life? What do you struggle with? What makes you rejoice?" Then it helps you read the Scriptures to discover their deep, abiding truths. IMMERSION is about God and God's Word, and it is also about you—not just your thoughts, but your feelings and your faith.

In each study you will prayerfully read the Scripture and reflect on it. Then you will engage it in three ways:

Claim Your Story
> Through stories and questions, think about your life, with its struggles and joys.

Enter the Bible Story
> Explore Scripture and consider what God is saying to you.

Live the Story
> Reflect on what you have discovered, and put it into practice in your life.

IMMERSION makes use of an exciting new translation of Scripture, the Common English Bible (CEB). The CEB and IMMERSION BIBLE STUDIES will offer adults:

- the emotional expectation to find the love of God
- the rational expectation to find the knowledge of God
- reliable, genuine, and credible power to transform lives
- clarity of language

Whether you are using the Common English Bible or another translation, IMMERSION BIBLE STUDIES will offer a refreshing plunge into God's Word, your life, and your life with God.

1.

Practical Wisdom

James 1:1–2:26

Claim Your Story

Think back for a few minutes to a time when, as a child or teenager, you did something wrong and were tempted to blame your action on somebody else. How about as an adult—ever face that temptation then?

Just as I was turning six years old my family moved from the green, lush hills of Tennessee to the desert of southern Arizona. As an only child I had to find ways to entertain myself. We were living in a trailer on a barren lot with one tree in the entire neighborhood and a drainage ditch at the bottom of the street on which we lived. One day I discovered the water meter, a round metal gauge and cap. When I got bored with simply opening and closing it, I decided to experiment with this new toy. I found that you could place the small sandy stones that lay around everywhere between the meter's cap and the metal base and crush the stone. After having crushed several stones I pressed the cap down and heard something that sounded like breaking glass. When I raised the cap I discovered that the rock I was trying to crush had slipped off the metal rim of the meter and broken the glass face.

I didn't tell anyone what had happened, but I overheard my dad and mom talking about the broken meter. The water company was going to pay to replace it because we hadn't broken it. After several days I told my father what had happened. When he asked why I was breaking rocks using the meter, I had no answer. Years later I might have borrowed the line from comedian Flip Wilson, "The devil made me do it." Still I knew that wasn't true. It would never have occurred to me to blame God, as the Letter of James suggests that some people did. I knew that it was my own boredom and my choices that broke the meter. My dad called the water company and told them that we would pay for the meter to be replaced.

From this experience I learned that I can't shift blame for my own actions onto anyone else, least of all God. I learned, also, that honesty and integrity are about doing the right thing, not just talking about it. The writer of James would agree.

Enter the Bible Story

The Letter of James is a book of the Bible that has been extremely important for some Christians through the ages and virtually neglected by others. Some accepted it readily because they believed that it had been written by the James who is named in the Gospels as the brother of Jesus. Others have suggested that someone else wrote the letter and put the name, James, on it. It could be that this is another writer named James or that they named it after James the brother of Jesus because they wanted people to take it seriously or to acknowledge that they had been a student of James's teaching. This was a common practice in the ancient world. Today we publish and copyright our words and thoughts and put our names on the book cover. In the ancient world, however, it would have been considered the height of arrogance for me to write down ideas that I might have learned from another, then attach my name to it. In addition, it might attract more readers if the name of someone better known than I am was on the letter. In any case, the writer of the Letter of James was a product of the early Christian communities, was probably very familiar with the Septuagint (the commonly used Greek translation of the Hebrew Bible), and was adept at the writing of *koine* Greek (the commonly spoken Greek at the time of Jesus and the years following).

Martin Luther was not very fond of the Letter of James. He is reported to have called it "an epistle of straw." He felt that the letter contradicted his own view that we are saved by grace working through faith. Luther seemed to feel that James's emphasis on works was a direct challenge to his own faith-based view of salvation. While this has been the dominant view of the letter in some circles, others defend the book's theology. To them it is simply a common-sense approach requiring believers to practice what we preach.

So the Letter of James stands right at the center of the ongoing conversation about whether those who would follow Jesus are called to a set of beliefs or a way of life. James clearly understands the need for belief, since he challenges certain misconceptions, like the idea that God could cause us to sin. Still, he argues strenuously that the life of faith is not simply giving assent to a certain set of beliefs. Unless we treat each other, especially those who are less fortunate, in a way that honors God by following the teachings of Jesus, professions of faith are empty. Even today there are those who will tell you that all one has to do to be a Christian is to believe a certain set of doctrinal statements, such as those contained in the historic creeds. Others contend that simply stating that one believes in Jesus as one's personal savior is sufficient for salvation. James could not disagree more!

Many scholars have noticed that the Letter of James is not typical of the epistles found in Scripture. The letter lacks certain features that readers have come to expect of letters, whether written to an individual or a community. It simply states who the writer is and to whom the remarks are addressed. Then it plunges right into the substance that the writer wants to communicate. There is no word of thanksgiving or blessing, and there is no expression of grace and peace to the readers. This has led some scholars to suggest that what we have here is not a letter at all, but a kind of essay or collection of short essays.

If the Letter of James is an essay, it seems at first to be a very disjointed one. Chapter 1 opens with a series of statements that at first glance seem to have no relation to each other. Is this a book like Proverbs that simply lists one wisdom saying after the other with little or no concern about continuity? James does seem intent on communicating a kind of wisdom, but it is wisdom that is less concerned with right belief than right action.

James's Poetic Prologue

It might help us understand the opening of this letter if we see it as poetry rather than prose. In our modern world we are so used to reading a letter or essay set in paragraphs that it is easy to forget that in the ancient world poetry was an important form in which wisdom could be expressed. The Book of Proverbs is poetry, as is most of the Book of Job. In many circumstances, writers in both the Hebrew Bible and the New Testament used poetic forms to express wisdom. That may be because much of the wisdom in the Bible had been passed along in the oral tradition for many years before it was written down.

If we divide these first verses of James into poetic lines, the passage seems less disjointed and begins to make poetic sense

In Hebrew poetry the lines do not rhyme as some English poems do. Rather, Hebrew poetry is structured around the repetition of ideas. This poetic form is called *parallelism*. An idea is stated in one line, then it is restated in a slightly different form in the following line.

For example, in Proverbs 8:32-36 the figure of Wisdom is speaking. She tells those who would be wise:

> Now children, listen to me:
>> Happy are those who keep to my ways!
> Listen to instruction, and be wise;
>> don't avoid it.
> Happy are those who listen to me,
>> watching daily at my doors,
>> waiting at my doorposts.
> Those who find me find life;
>> they gain favor from the LORD.
> Those who offend me
>> injure themselves;
>> all those who hate me love death.

The repetition serves in this passage to reinforce that a happy life is grounded in listening to the voice of Wisdom. The third line "listen to instruction" repeats "listen to me" in the first line; "don't avoid it" (wisdom) reinforces "keep to my ways." As you read through the passage you will note that this structure repeats itself until it reaches the final two lines, which restate the theme in the form of a warning to those who would not "listen" or "hear" Wisdom's voice, who did not "keep" but did "neglect" Wisdom's ways.

This same poetic parallel structure is at work if we divide the first verses of James into poetic lines.

> Wisdom will certainly be given to those who ask.
>> Whoever asks shouldn't hesitate.
>>> They should ask in faith without doubting.
> Whoever doubts is like the surf of the sea, tossed and turned by the wind.
>> People like that should never imagine that they will receive anything from the Lord.
>>> They are double-minded, unstable in all their ways.
>>> (James 1:5b-8)

The first set of three lines all speak to the issue of faith and doubt, each line reinforcing the idea stated in the line above it. The second set of three lines restates the issue employing a shadow or negative image that describes the person who does not participate in the wisdom outlined in the first three lines.

We see the same structure at work later in the first chapter when the writer states:

> No one who is tested should say, "God is tempting me!"
>> This is because God is not tempted by any form of evil,
>>> nor does he tempt anyone.
> Everyone is tempted by their own cravings; they are lured away and enticed by them.
>> Once those cravings conceive, they give birth to sin;
>>> and when sin grows up, it gives birth to death. (James 1:13-15)

The Letter of James as a Rule of Life

Everyone lives by some set of guidelines, stated or unstated. There are rules of the classroom and the workplace. There are practices that prepare us to play for sports or participate in the performing arts, and there are rules that govern our behavior when we take part in these activities. What if we read James as a rule of life that intends to describe those practices that lead to a healthy Christian community? James is a book of wisdom, but its wisdom is grounded in the practicalities of daily life in a community that claims to follow the teachings and example of Jesus. The writer wants us to listen to wisdom, then act on what we have heard.

This intent becomes clear toward the end of Chapter 1, which baldly states, "You must be doers of the word and not only hearers who mislead themselves" (James 1:22). Those who hear wisdom only and don't follow up that hearing with action are likely to forget, and having forgotten, don't even recognize themselves when they look into a mirror. The writer seems to imply that those who simply hear and don't act on what they hear can-

---

About the Christian Faith

The Rule of Benedict

In the late fourth and early fifth centuries, a layman named Benedict of Nursia wrote down a short list of guidelines by which Christian communities could live. You may wonder why such a list was needed. By this time Christianity was not only tolerated but was the state religion of Rome. The problem was that the Christian church had become identified with the Roman Empire and that empire was in the process of collapsing. Would Christianity go down with it?

For some time before Benedict appeared, Christians had been leaving the cities of the Empire and creating communities in the desert areas, mostly in Egypt. Some of these communities had begun to develop guides for living together commonly called "Rules." The Rule of Benedict is the only one of those guides for life together that is still used by communities to this day. With the Rule divided into daily readings, each monastic community reads through the Rule three times during the year. Not only do the members of these communities read it, they order their lives around its instruction.

not even recognize the very self that God created them to be. Any teacher will tell you that we will remember a very small portion of what we hear, a little more of what we read, but a great deal more of those things in which we actively participate.

James can be described as a rule of life for those who would follow Jesus. This is the reason the writer focuses on practices, what Christians actually do, rather than what they believe.

In recent years there has been a lot of conversation around Christian practices. A practice is not something that we do once or only occasionally. A Christian practice is an action that we do again and again as part of the discipline that helps us live as disciples of Jesus. Anything we do habitually forms us spiritually. If we continuously gossip or complain, those practices form us spiritually, and not for the better! If we pray and attempt to return good for evil, both of which Jesus specifically practiced and told us to do, we are formed into the likeness of Jesus. This is what we as Christians want to happen. So we ask ourselves, what are those things I do habitually that bring me closer to the way Jesus lived, and what are those practices that lead me farther away from that example Jesus set for us?

This is not a modern problem, that people practice actions that remove them from the life of faith. James mentions several practices that lead people away from Jesus—not holding their tongues and attending to the wealthy more than the poor, for example. In addition, the writer outlines those practices that are described as doing the truth and that lead us closer to the likeness of Jesus.

Live the Story

Not playing favorites is one of the most difficult things in the world. How can parents whose children are radically different not prefer the one who is compliant to the one who is rebellious? What parent will not defer to the child who is more like that parent? Scripture depicts both the devastating results of such favoritism and the way God can use this human disposition to choose one child over the other in the story of Jacob and Esau. Jacob is Rachel's favorite son. After all, he sits in the tent and talks recipes with her. Esau, on the other hand, loves the outdoors, especially hunting, and is his father's favorite. This practice of parental favoritism leads to an (almost) deadly hatred between the two brothers, which is resolved only after many years of exile when Jacob returns to encounter Esau.

Favoritism was clearly an issue among the early followers of Jesus. Otherwise why would James place such an emphasis on choosing not to favor members of wealth and position over the poor? This still seems to be an issue for the followers of Jesus today. How do you and your congregation promote or resist showing favoritism toward those who are already privileged?

A congregation I served some years ago helped a homeless man who had a prison record and invited him to attend worship. At first, the visitor seemed to attend worship only for what he could get out of it. (In truth, sometimes we "respectable" people attend worship for the same reason.) He would disappear for weeks at a time only to reappear needing help again. Over the years the congregation received our "guest" just like any other member. With the help of several families he was able to get his life together. After a while he was invited to serve as an usher. Not everyone was happy with this decision, but soon our "guest" had become a part of the family. Today that congregation would consider itself deprived if he were not a part of their life together.

Is this what James is talking about? What is your congregation doing to live this story?

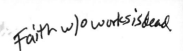
Faith w/o works is dead

gossip envy

2.

Worldly Values and Wisdom From Above

good

James 3:1–5:20

gossip & story

Claim Your Story

Have you ever been the victim of gossip? Have you ever caused someone else harm by passing along, or not challenging, gossip?

There is a story told about a rabbi who lived in Eastern Europe roughly three hundred years ago. A member of that community who was a terrible gossip was sent to this particular rabbi who was well known for helping people break destructive habits.

When the gossip arrived he attempted to defend passing along unsubstantiated rumors: "These are only words, after all. How much harm can words do?"

"Have you attempted to determine if the words are true before you passed them along?" questioned the rabbi.

"Not exactly," replied the gossip, "but if they should prove to be untrue I will just take them all back."

"You'll take them all back, will you?" the rabbi asked. "Wait here."

Momentarily the rabbi returned with a feather pillow in which he had cut a hole at one end. The gossip followed the rabbi outside. The rabbi gave the gossip the feather pillow with the instruction to fling it as hard as possible in all directions. Feathers flew everywhere. The breeze picked up some and carried them into nearby streets and alleys as well as over the rooftops of neighboring houses.

After the feathers had scattered throughout the village and beyond, the rabbi turned to the gossip and said, "Now go collect all those feathers for me so I can put them back in my pillow."

The gossip was astounded that the rabbi would make such a ridiculous request.

"That's impossible." The gossip was clearly frustrated.

"True," the rabbi agreed, "and it is just as impossible for you to take back all the words you have scattered throughout the village and beyond once they have flown out of your mouth."

Most of us learned this ditty as children: "Sticks and stones may break my bones, but words will never hurt me." We soon learned that this bit of common wisdom was rarely true. Words do hurt. Words can do damage. It is just that the wounds and bruises they leave behind are not as visible.

James counsels us to tame the tongue at the same time he acknowledges how difficult that can be for most people. Words spoken for ill or good are impossible to contain once they are set free into the world.

Enter the Bible Story

A Word to the Wise

Chapter 3 of James opens with what appears to be an odd warning: "Not many of you should become teachers, because we know that we teachers will be judged more strictly" (James 1:3). How do you think that approach would work with your children's ministry program during teacher recruitment time in your congregation? The children's council at the church I serve would be up in arms if I preached that!

Why would the writer of this letter place such a responsibility on the heads of teachers? Perhaps it is because teachers use so many words and words can be such powerful forces for good or harm. If there is any doubt about the power of language, just look at the partial truths, distortions, and outright lies that are part and parcel of every political campaign. These are intended to gain advantage for one candidate. Too often even we Christians allow such tactics to go unchallenged, especially if they benefit the candidate we support. James will have none of that!

According to James there is one part of the body that is more dangerous than any other, and it is not the one most people would suspect! The tongue is a dangerous weapon according to James. Many of us have a difficult time believing this, until we remember the last time we lashed out at someone in anger and saw the devastation reflected in their face. First, tongues produce words and words are like horses, the letter says. They need to be bridled, kept under control. Otherwise we are tempted to jump on that horse and ride off in all directions. James makes the astonishing assertion that the tongue controls one's whole body. If the tongue runs wild the entire person is in jeopardy.

Second, words are like a ship. If they have no one to pilot them, to direct their course, they have no direction and wind up crashing into the rocks. The theme James lifts up here is boasting. The speaker needs to have a strong rudder and to keep an even keel in order to avoid boasting. This is a timely caution in a day of résumé inflation (or sometimes misrepresentation) even among well-known writers, scholars, and professionals.

Third, a word can act like a small flame that sets an entire forest on fire. We read about such situations each year. A neglected campfire or an arsonist with just such a small flame begins a wildfire that burns thousands of acres, and often homes as well. Our words can be just as destructive, whether we intend them to be or not. The tongue "is a restless evil, full of deadly poison. With it we both bless the Lord and Father and curse human beings made in God's likeness" (3:8b-9).

Use tongue to bless & curse

What could the followers of Jesus have been saying about each other that would have elicited such a passionate response? We don't know for sure, but they could have been making the same sorts of accusations that Christians have made against other Christians through the ages—and still do today. Take note: James does not condemn evil and poisonous words against other believers alone, but includes every human being made in God's likeness. This rule of life for the followers of Jesus prohibits hurtful and slanderous words aimed at anyone, since all humans are created in the image of God. We cannot bless God and curse anyone if we truly represent the community that Jesus has called to follow his example. Strong stuff here!

Sometimes we Christians utter poisonous words with the best of intentions. Several years ago a friend, a committed Christian, forwarded an e-mail to me that contained scurrilous accusations against a major international company, including the claim that its trademark was a demonic symbol and that the CEO was a Satan worshiper. To verify these claims the e-mail stated that the CEO had admitted as much on a nationally televised talk show, even giving the date of the broadcast.

It took less than five minutes to find that the date listed in the e-mail was a Sunday, a day of the week that this particular talk show was not broadcast. A little more searching on Internet hoax websites indicated that the accusations were rumors that had been passed along for years and had never been true.

My friend had forwarded the e-mail with the best of intentions, to protect fellow Christians from becoming entangled with a Satan worshiper. Even so, because the words contained in the e-mail about the company and its CEO were patently untrue, instead of doing great good great harm could have been done. The tongue, the pencil, the computer, the smartphone, or anything else that generates words can be an evil and poisonous weapon and must be used with great care . . . and great caring. This is the warning that James is trying to convey.

The High and the Mighty

The section beginning with James 3:13 is addressed to anyone who is "wise and understanding," counseling them to "show that your actions are good with a humble lifestyle that comes from wisdom." Here the writer states his intention for this rule of life that is being shared with communities torn by envy and jealousy, pride and arrogance, and showing favoritism toward the wealthy. The goal of James's rule is to describe what life can be like when it is lived according to "wisdom from above." Such a life and the characteristics of a community that lives by such a rule of life are: "First, it is pure, and then peaceful, gentle, obedient, filled with mercy and good actions, fair, and genuine. Those who make peace sow the seeds of justice by their peaceful acts" (3:17).

Across the Testaments

Wisdom as a Way of Life

The theme of _wisdom_ is prominent in James (see 1:5-8; 3:13-18). For James, true wisdom is not a matter of the head but of behavior. Wisdom has less to do with having good ideas and more to do with living good lives.

Attention to wisdom in the Letter of James echoes Proverbs, one of three books of wisdom in the Old Testament (the others are Job and Ecclesiastes). Like James, wisdom in Proverbs is not an intellectual matter but a way of living in relationship to God.

The LORD gives wisdom;
   from his mouth come knowledge and understanding.
He reserves ability for those with integrity.
   He is a shield for those who live a blameless life.
He protects the paths of justice
   and guards the way of those who are loyal to him.
Then you will understand righteousness and justice,
   as well as integrity, every good course.
Wisdom will enter your mind,
   and knowledge will fill you with delight.
Discretion will guard you;
   understanding will protect you. (Proverbs 2:6-11)

I teach you the path of wisdom.
   I lead you in straight courses.
When you walk, you won't be hindered;
   when you run, you won't stumble.
Hold on to instruction; don't slack off;
   protect it, for it is your life. (Proverbs 4:11-13)

The Letter of James contrasts the lives of those who are wise and understanding with lives of those formed by the values of the world: envy, jealousy, pride, and arrogance—all of which are linked in the mind of the writer of James with wealth. In the world people are taught to want what others have. We envy others and become jealous of them because we don't have what they have, and we want to have it. In our modern world this seems to be the very purpose of advertising, to cultivate envy and jealousy that will motivate people to buy things they see others enjoying, whether they need them or not. The worldly life is one in which we can only feel better about ourselves if we can judge others as inferior to us. We are supposed to live in the best zip codes, drive the most expensive automobile, and send our children to the most prestigious schools. Such pride, such arrogance is not from above but from below—this world—and thus is beneath the standard expected of the followers of Jesus.

These warnings, as well as the rule of life that James sets forth, seem to be especially pertinent in our time. In the twenty-first century it can cost many millions of dollars to run for political office. Though politicians frequently deny it, we all know that many of those donations come from individuals and groups who want to influence the way that elected official will vote on issues that affect the donors. In recent years, we have seen people develop financial schemes that placed at risk the savings and retirement funds entrusted to them while assuring their own continuing enrichment.

We might wonder, "Where is James when we need him?" Well, this letter is still in the Bible and, though often ignored, it still has a word of wisdom for our day and time. It is said that money talks; and some have even defined the Golden Rule, which was originally stated as, "Treat people in the same way that you want them to treat you" (Luke 6:31), to mean, "The ones who have the gold make the rules." A story I heard from my father as I was growing up told of a father who was giving business advice to his son. "Make the dollar," the father counseled, "honestly, if you can. If not, make the dollar." My dad, who was the son of a tenant farmer and an automobile mechanic, meant it as a cautionary tale. There were people in the world who would make money by any means, no matter what they had to say or do to get it. I was not to grow up to be one of those people.

Sometimes, especially in religious settings, arrogance can be touted as a virtue. A folk tale demonstrates that we can even mistake one of the vices described in the Letter of James for its opposite virtue. During the prayer time in a particular religious service, a well-dressed man stood up and prayed aloud, "Though I own ships that sail the seven seas and barns to store all my goods, I am nothing in the sight of God." Then he sat down. Soon after, another man stood and prayed aloud, "Though I have more ships than the man who just prayed and bigger barns that hold more goods than his, I am nothing in the sight of God." A short time later a very poor man, a beggar, stood and began to pray aloud, "Though I have never seen a ship, and I sleep in barns . . ." The two men who had prayed previously stood and said to the beggar, "Sit down and be quiet. You're not important enough to be nothing in the sight of God."

Wealth is not evil in and of itself, but it does present a danger to the one who would be wise in God's ways. The desire for wealth and the things we can acquire with it is too often fueled by envy and leads to arrogance. Perhaps even a greater danger is that people begin to think they can never have enough and they can (and should) buy anything and everything regardless of their true need. Such people want to be in control of their world, to possess everything in that world. They want their lives to be predictable—the stock market will always go up and never down, their investments will always produce returns and they will never suffer losses, they will never lose a job or have a relationship fall apart or suffer grief at the loss of a loved one. If other people get hurt along the way or are deprived of the necessities of life, well, that is just the price of doing business. Wealth and the desire to accumulate can lead to the attitude that there is no need to care for the needs of those less fortunate than ourselves. Of course, not all wealthy people succumb to these "worldly temptations," nor are envy and pride limited to the wealthy. Still, according to James, for those who claim to be followers of the teaching and example of Jesus, wealth can be a clear and present danger.

Patience and Prayer

Finally, the Letter of James counsels those who read it to be patient. Even then they were wondering why God had not come and set things right. Across the years people have asked me, don't you think it's the end time? Look at all the terrible things that are going on around us, wars and terrorism, earthquakes and tornadoes and hurricanes. We are still impatient. After all, it has been many centuries since James assured his readers, "the Lord is near" (5:8b). Some of us become so impatient that we devise elaborate schemes for determining the date of the "coming of the Lord." These invariably pass without incident. We are not called to predict the day but to wait with patience for its coming. "Don't complain about each other . . ." (5:9), we are counseled, ". . . for the Lord is full of compassion and mercy" (5:11).

So what are we to do while we wait patiently? James suggests that we pray. Instead of complaining about our neighbors, James exhorts us to confess our own sins. This is a practice that is intended to break down the arrogance against which the letter warns and to create in us humble hearts. Confession helps us follow Jesus' instruction to take the log out of our own eye before we worry about the splinter in our neighbor's eye (Matthew 7:3-5; Luke 6:41-42). Instead of employing our tongues as weapons, we should use them to cleanse our hearts and minds of the thoughts, words, and actions that harm ourselves and others. "For this reason, confess your sins to each other and pray for each other so that you may be healed" (James 5:16).

In addition, we are called to pray for those who are in need of healing, of body, mind, or spirit. "If any of you are sick, they should call for the elders of the church, and the elders should pray over them, anointing them with oil in the name of the Lord" (5:14). Many churches have established prayers for healing as a part of certain ones or all of their services of Holy Communion. Sometimes teams of church members will go to the home of someone who is ill, anoint them, and pray for them. Rarely do any of these teams experience miraculous cures like those featured on certain televisions programs. Remember, not a single person

Jesus healed is still around today. All of them died at some point after their healing encounter with Jesus.

I was part of just such a service for a friend and parishioner some years ago. There was no miraculous cure. He lived for about a year after our visit and the prayers for healing and anointing. During that year he was reconciled to both his son and his brother. They were both at his side when he died. I would suggest that my friend died a healed man.

Live the Story

What do you think James would say if he could watch just one evening of so-called "reality television"? Perhaps just what the letter says about the dangers of the tongue and hurtful words. Or how would the growing divide between the rich and poor in our country and across the world strike this ancient follower of Jesus? Would we hear the same words of warning that are already in the letter about envy, pride, and the difference between the way we treat the wealthy and the way we treat the poor?

Could this letter provide a rule of life for our churches today? Have modern congregations gotten caught up in the standards of the world, measuring success by the size of our membership rolls or our budgets, rather than by the quality of our relationship with God and our neighbor?

We might outline such a rule of life in this way:

1. Everything is a gift from God—we did not earn nor can we deserve either who we are or what we have.
2. Treat everyone as a beloved child of God, no matter what their place in society. Neither speak ill of them nor treat them badly.
3. Put flesh on words of faith by performing acts of compassion for those less fortunate.
4. Speak no evil of anyone because our words can be weapons of destruction.
5. Be generous not envious; be humble not arrogant, and if you have wealth do not view it as anything other than a tool through which to serve God and your neighbor.

6. Be patient, and have courage. During even the most difficult times God is with you.

to offset dangers: prayer + Confessions

For James the antidote to the dangers of this world include prayer, specifically prayers for others and confession of our sins. If our congregations followed this simple rule of life set forth by the Letter of James, might we not become pure, peaceful, gentle, obedient, merciful, good in our acts toward others, fair, and genuine? Might we then embody the wisdom that comes from above, wisdom that is a gift from God alone?

3.

A Life of Grateful Obedience

1 Peter 1:1–2:12

Claim Your Story

As I was growing up in a rural area of the South, my parents took it upon themselves to teach me manners. I am not talking about setting the table in the proper way or which fork with which to eat my salad. The manners I learned had to do with the way I was expected to interact with other people.

As archaic as it may seem to many young people today, I was taught to say, "Yes, sir" and "Yes, ma'am" to adults. I would not have simply answered, "Yes," and certainly never, "Yeah." The same was true with, "No, sir" and "No, ma'am." In fact, even today I find myself employing those same manners with adults who are younger than I am.

When we asked for something, we were expected to say, "Please." When we were given a gift, or our plate was served at the dinner table, or someone complimented us, we were expected to say, "Thank you." If those responses were not immediately forthcoming, one of my parents would ask, "What do you say?" Whereupon I was expected to offer the proper response. At the same time I was being taught to express my gratitude, I was being taught to be obedient.

Take a minute to play "free association." What comes to mind when you hear the word *obedience*? Are the connotations positive? Negative? What history does the concept of obedience have for you personally?

The opening passages of First Peter have to do with gratitude, specifically for what God has done for us and all people through Jesus Christ. The gratitude described here goes far beyond a simple "Thank you." God calls us to a life of thankfulness, a life soaked through with gratitude. We are even to be grateful for those times of trial and suffering that come along in each life, because they give an opportunity to follow the example of Jesus.

If we look at the First Letter of Peter through the lens of gratitude, it makes clear statements that foreshadow points the writer will make throughout the letter. For the writer of First Peter gratitude and obedience go hand in hand. We are obedient because we are grateful, and we are grateful because we have seen the obedience of Jesus and want to emulate him in our lives.

Enter the Bible Story

Grateful Obedience

The Prayer of Confession and Pardon in the Service of Word and Table of The United Methodist Church includes a profoundly important request of God. After confessing all those things we had failed to do as a community of faith and asking forgiveness from God, the prayer has the words, "Free us for joyful obedience" (*The United Methodist Hymnal*, page 8). For many people in our time the words *joyful* and *obedience* standing side by side makes no sense at all. We have come to believe as a culture that to be truly joyful we have to be free to do whatever we want. The very word, *obedience*, leaves a bad taste in our mouths, because to be obedient to anyone seems to be an infringement on that very freedom that as individuals makes us joyful.

The writer of First Peter takes just the opposite view of the relationship between joy and obedience. In this letter gratitude, which is the fruit of obedience, is the source of joy; unchecked individual freedom was seen as license and was condemned. That may be why those to whom the letter is addressed are called "strangers," or as the New Revised Standard Version translates it, "exiles." Not only are they living among a people not their own, as followers of Jesus, they are living by a set of values that is sharply different from the culture surrounding them.

It might be helpful here to distinguish between *joy* and *happiness*. Most of us say we want to be happy and we want those we love to be happy. The problem is that happiness depends on the circumstances of our lives. If things are going well for us, then we are happy. If things are not going well in our lives, if a relationship dissolves, or a job disappears, or a loved one dies, then we are unhappy. Joy is different though. It does not depend upon circumstances. Rather, joy is dependent upon our recognition of God's loving and graceful presence with us through the times when things are going our way as well as the times when things seem to unravel. This may be why Paul writes in First Thessalonians, "Rejoice always. Pray continually. Give thanks in every situation" (1 Thessalonians 5:16-18a).

About the Scripture

The People to Whom This Letter Was Written

The people to whom First Peter is addressed lived in the Eastern provinces of the Roman Empire. They did not live near the center of political power (Rome) nor the center of religious power (Jerusalem). Rather they lived as part of the *diaspora*, a term that comes from a combination of two Greek words and means to scatter around. Originally it referred to Jews who had been scattered around the Empire. Later it came to be applied to any group of people dispersed from their original homeland.

While the use of this term might imply that all those for whom the letter was written were Jewish followers of Jesus, this does not seem to be the case. The writer seems to employ the term *diaspora* in the second of its meanings. Diaspora here seems to refer to all the followers of Jesus, many of whom now are Gentiles living among a general population of mostly Gentiles who are not followers of Jesus. Many of the believers may have literally been immigrants or guest workers, but it is their status as Jesus' followers that sets them apart within the surrounding culture.

Our primary clue about the people to whom this letter was written is that the majority were Gentile. "Once you weren't a people, but now you are God's people. Once you hadn't received mercy, but now you have received mercy" (1 Peter 2:10). The indication is that those reading the letter had been adopted into the people of God. If it were addressed primarily to a Jewish readership this would make no sense. They would have already considered themselves to be God's people before they chose to become followers of Jesus. Gentiles, on the other hand, would have been considered to be no people until they entered into the people of God through the gateway of Jesus.

Prayer keeps us aware of God's presence with us so we may rejoice and give thanks no matter what the circumstances of our lives may be.

The joy that these strangers in a strange land celebrate is grounded in something called "new birth." They have been "born anew into a living hope through the resurrection of Jesus Christ from the dead" (1 Peter 1:3). The hope described here, unlike what people commonly define as hope, will last. They "have a pure and enduring inheritance that cannot perish." The fact that they can "rejoice in this hope" is all the more significant because they are apparently "distressed for a short time by various trials" (1:6). Such distressing occasions are all for the good because by enduring them "your faith may be found genuine" (1:7).

Deep and lasting joy emerges from gratitude for what Jesus has done, though none of those hearing this letter read aloud were among his original followers. "Although you've never seen him, you love him. Even though you don't see him now, you trust him and so rejoice with a glorious joy that is too much for words" (1:8). The people who heard this letter were apparently among those whom Jesus refers to as "sheep that don't belong to this sheep pen" (John 10:16). Jesus describes these same followers to an astounded Thomas as joyful. "Happy are those who don't see me and yet believe" (John 20:29).

For the writer of First Peter this living hope culminating in Jesus began with the prophets. Even though the prophets didn't know they were talking about the person of Jesus, when reading those texts through the lens of Jesus and the new birth he brings, the writer of First Peter recognizes both the person and the era of which they spoke. That is why he can say of the prophets: "in their search they were not serving themselves but you" (1 Peter 1:12).

Such gratitude inevitably leads those who follow Jesus into a life of obedience. By being obedient to the living hope, they set themselves apart from the culture around them. In other words, they become holy, set apart for the purposes of God. Holiness is the fruit of a life lived in gratitude for all that God has done and a willing and joyful obedience to all that God calls us to be and do. Today we often shy away from the word *holy*. To modern ears it smacks of self-righteousness or a holier-than-thou attitude.

However, understood in its original meaning, "being set apart," it can help us appreciate the situation of those who would have heard this letter. Many were set apart as "strangers" in a part of the world that was not their place of origin. They were all intended to be set apart by their gratitude and obedience to God and the joy these bring with them.

Imagining a Life of Joyful Obedience

In the first ten verses of Chapter 2, the writer employs a chain of linked images to describe what such joyful hope and grateful obedience looks like. These are: stone-temple-race-priesthood-nation-people of God. In choosing this string of images, the writer is giving us a number of ways of imagining what a life of joyful obedience would look like.

First we are stones. We are stones that are to be set apart by God, much like the stones used in building a place of worship. Even though we are rejected by others we are still useful to God. Every person is valuable in God's building project. We are not lifeless stones, but living stones. While lifeless stones are useful in building a physical structure like a temple, living stones are to be used when a spiritual temple is what one has in mind. That is exactly what God has in mind. This community, through their living hope, and their lives of gratitude and joyful obedience have become the living stones with which God builds a spiritual temple. How might our congregations be described as "living stones" and our communities as "spiritual temples"?

Now the Temple at Jerusalem was the central place of Jewish worship. Even though there were synagogues in local communities during Jesus' time and after, the Temple was the place where the sacrifices were made and the high holy days were to be observed. As an observant Jew, Jesus spent time with his followers at the Temple. Even though he did not agree with everything that went on there (his overturning the tables of the moneychangers is one example, Mark 11:15-19), he still chose to teach there and acknowledged that it was intended to be a true place of worship (Mark 11:17).

First Peter uses the term *temple* in a very different way. The temple, for First Peter, is not a building. Rather it is a people. The people who heard this letter lived far from Jerusalem and the Temple. It would appear that many, if not most of them, were Gentiles for whom the Jewish Temple would have little meaning. It is possible that this letter was composed after the Temple had been destroyed. So, even for those Jews who would read the letter, the Temple would likely be just a memory. The temple in this letter is one that God is building from the living stones (people) that are assembled into a temple (community). This temple is not limited by time and space, but is a movable feast so that worship can take place whenever and wherever the community gathers.

The third image extends and deepens the first two. Though most of the people to whom he writes are not Jewish, the writer calls them "a chosen race." Some have interpreted the use of this image to suggest that the followers of Jesus have replaced the Jews as God's chosen people. I think, rather, that the writer is suggesting that all the races of the earth are chosen; all we have to do is respond to our having been chosen. This does not diminish the role that the Jewish people continue to play in God's drama that is taking place in and for the world, but it extends the cast of characters to practically anyone who is willing to take a part.

Next, the people are called a royal priesthood. Here again, the concepts of both royalty and priesthood are extended beyond their normal usage. Both royalty and priesthood have previously been restricted to only certain groups who, by military might or family heritage, have qualified for those positions of honor. In the world that God is bringing into being, everyone qualifies as royalty, without having to be born into a certain family or lead a conquering army. Likewise, priesthood is extended to all who will participate in grateful, joyful obedience in response to God's good gifts. The doors of royalty and priesthood, which had been locked to the vast majority of people before, are thrown open to the world.

I suggested in Chapter 1 that the prologue of James could be read fruitfully as poetry instead of prose. Let me offer here my own poetic way of expressing what the writer of First Peter is saying about the life of joyful obedience. I call this poem "From Dead Dry Rocks."

From dead dry rocks
Living stones are born
To build a temple worthy
Of the breath of God.

From ordinary folk
A priesthood is formed
Every one a royal heir
To this place of grace.

From no people
God's people are formed
A holy nation
The possession of God.

From dead dry rocks
Living stones are born
To build a temple
Whose doors are open to the world.

The image of a holy nation is akin to that of a chosen people, an image that could be interpreted as a replacement of the Jewish people. In the context of this series of poetic images, however, it forms a new vision of how God works. As Peter stated as he stood just across the threshold of the house of Cornelius, a Gentile and a Roman officer: "I am really learning that God doesn't show partiality to one group of people over another. Rather, in every nation, whoever worships him and does what is right is acceptable to him" (Acts 10:34-35). God does not choose just one people; God chooses all people. The question, then, is: will we respond to God's having chosen us to be a part of the drama named "Shalom"? The word *shalom* means more than peace; it represents the way God intended the world to be from the beginning, which certainly includes peace and much, much more. We realize that we are "a people who are God's own possession" (1 Peter 2:9) as we participate in God's dream for the world and its people. In Jesus, the doors to becoming God's people are thrown open wide. The only way we are excluded is if we refuse to respond in joyful obedience and exclude ourselves.

All this is a hopeful message for those who would be considered strangers and exiles, whom others might exclude because they don't fit in to the majority culture. God has chosen all people for royalty, priesthood, and holy community. All people are invited to respond and take part in what God is doing in and through these new communities. Of course, this actually could mean trouble for those who are considered outsiders if their behavior is radically different from the culture around them. The writer addresses this issue in the rest of the letter.

Live the Story

How do we live a life of grateful obedience today? God's act of choosing all people to be a part of God's dream for the world has not been taken back. We too are invited to take a role in the drama that God is enacting in our time. Here are some practices that might help us live lives of joyful obedience. Which are you willing to do?

1. Begin each morning by thanking God for the day to come. Then end each day by thanking God for the day that has been and the rest night will bring.
2. Before going to sleep think back through the day and note the many blessings you have received during that day. In short, count (and name) your blessings.
3. Pass those blessings along. A few years ago there was a movie named *Pay It Forward*, which popularized this idea. Instead of paying back, we pay our blessings forward by passing along the good that we have experienced that day.
4. Picture each family member, co-worker, friend, and even (or maybe especially) those with whom we have had a disagreement. Ask, "What can I do to make that person's day better?"

5. Go through your closet, attic, garage, or other storage places and gather up the things you don't really need and give them away. That's right, don't sell them, give them away.

6. Read the story commonly called "The Good Samaritan" (Luke 10: 25-37). Try to imagine the story from the perspective of the person who has been beaten, robbed, and left to die by the side of the road. Then imagine the story from the perspective of the one who showed mercy.

7. Think back to the times when you have had troubles and someone reached out to you. Then ask, "Who is my neighbor?" and act accordingly.

8. Read the parable of the last judgment in Matthew 25:31-46. Note the lack of self-concern the sheep exhibit when they are told how they welcomed and offered help to others. Then take note of the self-interest of the goats who will only respond if they know that there is something to be gained for them in doing so. Who are you?

9. Ask who the least of these are in your community and our world. Be sheep to them.

10. Look for the presence of Jesus in your daily life. Follow him.

4.

Suffering Love

1 Peter 2:13–5:14

Claim Your Story

Undeserved suffering has been a potential result of the life of faith since there have been followers of Jesus. From the Roman Empire to Hitler's Reich to modern-day China, followers who tried to follow his example have found themselves being punished for doing the right thing. While Christians in other parts of the world still experience persecution, few of us who live in North America suffer for our faith.

When have you been accused and punished for something you didn't do? It might be a case as simple as an entire class of children being punished for something one of the students did. Or perhaps the surrounding cars are racing by you on the Interstate, placing you and your family in danger because you are driving at the posted speed limit. Or your boss asks you to do something for the company that you consider unethical and you refuse, then are fired as a result.

When have you heard of others who have suffered without deserving to? Examples of undeserved suffering might be as serious as a person who has lived on death row for many years being exonerated by DNA evidence that proved the inmate didn't commit the crime of which he or she was convicted. Or worse, sometimes evidence appears after an execution that the executed person was innocent. How are we as Christians to respond when we suffer when we have done nothing wrong? How do we respond when we see others suffering when they have done no wrong?

These are not new questions. The writer of this letter was very familiar with situations where followers of Jesus might suffer for something they didn't do or for choosing to do the right thing. After all everyone would have known the example of suffering love in the story of Jesus' passion, death, and resurrection.

Enter the Bible Story

The Blessing of Undeserved Suffering

The writer of First Peter is concerned that the followers of Jesus distinguish themselves from the culture around them, while at the same time getting along with their nonbelieving neighbors and the governing bodies under whose authority they live. Those reading this letter are aliens and strangers in more ways than one. Indications are that many are literally immigrants or guest workers and so considered outsiders to the local culture. In addition, their status as followers of Jesus sets them apart in even more distinct ways.

Given their status as outsiders they are warned against being punished justifiably for breaking the laws of the society in which they are living. They are counseled, "Live honorably among the unbelievers" (1 Peter 2:12). Even though they live honorably they will run the risk of being punished for crimes they didn't commit. This is an important distinction to the writer of this letter. There is no benefit to oneself or others when punishment comes as a result of wrongdoing. As people who are free to choose their actions, followers of Jesus are warned not to use "your freedom as a cover-up for evil" (2:16).

Undeserved punishment is a different matter altogether. "If you endure steadfastly when you've done good and suffer for it, this is commendable before God" (2:20). At first, this seems counterintuitive to those of us who read the letter today, as it very well may have to those who first read it. First Peter is picking up a theme that Jesus addresses in the Beatitudes: "Happy are you when people insult you and harass you and speak all kinds of bad and false things about you, all because of me. Be full of joy and be glad, because you have a great reward in heaven. In the same way, people harassed the prophets who came before you" (Matthew 5:11-12). Some translations say, "Blessed" or "Holy" in place of "Happy," but the general idea is the same. Followers of Jesus are to accept harsh words and treatment directed toward them for doing good because blessing, holiness, and happiness are found in following the example of the prophets and the teachings and example of Jesus.

There is an important by-product to such undeserved suffering, however. First Peter promises, "Today, they defame you, as if you were doing evil. But in the day when God visits to judge they will glorify him, because they have observed your honorable deeds" (1 Peter 2:12). The example of undeserved suffering accepted by the followers of Jesus without resorting to harsh words or treatment in return will be the very thing that will allow those who speak evil against them to glorify God on the Day of Judgment. In short, being punished for doing the right thing will be the means of conversion of others to a blessed, holy, and happy (blessed or holy) way of life, the way of Jesus.

Suffering and Submission

This idea of the blessedness of undeserved suffering lays the foundation for the writer's proposals about the power of submission. The words *submit* and *submission* describe a posture in relation to others that is not popular in today's world. These verses have lead to wrongheaded and even dangerous counsel to abused women simply to submit to the abuser. The danger here, as with many Bible passages, is that of picking out a text from the ancient world and applying it to current life situations without exploring the context in which it originally was written.

Every author is a product of a particular time and culture. This applies to the biblical writers as well as Shakespeare or Flannery O'Connor. The writer of First Peter was shaped by the practices and customs of the time during which the letter was written. The letter advises its readers,

For the sake of the Lord submit to every human institution. Do this whether this means submitting to the emperor as supreme ruler, or to governors as those sent by the emperor. They are sent to punish those doing evil and to praise those doing good. Submit to them because it's God's will that by doing good you will silence the ignorant talk of foolish people. (2:13-15)

At first this seems to be a complete capitulation to the powers that be. Is First Peter just expressing a "go along to get along" attitude, or is there something deeper going on here? This advice is clearly in line with the idea expressed earlier in the letter that followers of Jesus should avoid being punished for doing wrong, which here seems to be interpreted as breaking the laws of the human institutions in which they live. Apparently there were "foolish people" making accusations against the followers of Jesus based on ignorance and implying that they were disloyal to the emperor and his governors. It seems that the writer is encouraging the followers of Jesus to avoid even the appearance of being lawbreakers and even the possibility of being punished for wrongdoing. They are to be examples of law-abiding citizens for the surrounding culture.

Then the writer adds this, in many ways, subversive statement: "Do this as God's slaves, and yet also as free people" (2:16). Don't obey the law as a slave to any human institution or to any emperor or governor, but as one who serves the wishes of God. Anyone who does so, according to First Peter, is a truly free person. The freedom that comes from God is only to be employed to do good, never to do evil. As verse 17 makes clear, this God-given freedom allows the followers of Jesus to respect the emperor just as they are to respect everyone else, but fear (awe-inspired respect) is reserved for God alone. In other words, followers of Jesus do good not out of loyalty to the emperor or any governor or any human institution. Their motive is simply to be loyal to God and to please God.

First Peter does not challenge the institution of slavery, and this section of the writer's counsel seems to be clearly defined by the culture of its time. Slaves are simply to be obedient to their masters, even if their masters are unjust and treat them harshly. This obviously does not square with the modern conception of human rights and humane treatment for all people. No Christian (in fact, no compassionate person) today would make the argument that slavery should be reinstituted and that slaves should be expected to suffer harsh and unjust treatment.

Still, the counsel that is given to slaves here may just make sense within the culture of the time. Slaves were treated unjustly by some masters, even harshly. If they struck out against their masters in anger they

The Roman Family

The basic component of society within the Roman Empire was the family. The modern concept of family should not be the basis for our understanding of the family structures addressed in First Peter. Families of the Empire in that age were not formed so much around blood relations, although wives and children did play a part in it. Wayne Meeks summarizes research on the nature of the Roman household this way: " 'Family' is defined not first by kinship but by the relationship of dependence and subordination. The head of a substantial household was thus responsible for—and expected a degree of obedience from—not only his immediate family but also his slaves, former slaves who were now clients, hired laborers, and sometimes business associates or tenants."[1] Households were built around "the relationships of authority and subordination between three pairs: husbands and wives, fathers and children (mothers often are not mentioned), and masters and slaves."[2] According to Plutarch, for example, the husband's role was to rule and the wife's role was to be subordinate. Slaves were clearly subordinate to the head of the household and perhaps to other members of the family as well. Slaves were considered a part of the extended household, which meant that they had a place in the hierarchy of dependence and submission that was the Roman family.

could be punished severely, even put to death. To submit or not to such treatment could mean the difference between life and death for a slave. What the writer of First Peter does, interestingly enough, is to put human suffering in the context of Christ's suffering. When a slave suffers—having done nothing wrong—then the slave is following the example of Jesus who suffered though he had done nothing wrong. The writer might not be able to prevent or put an end to slaves' suffering, but these words reflect a serious attempt to give meaning to innocent suffering. Perhaps these verses were intended to provide slaves with a larger narrative of unjust suffering into which they could place the injustice they experience. It is a story in which God, not the slave master, has the final word.

Perhaps a twentieth-century example will help here. In 1946, Viktor Frankl published a book based on his experiences in the Nazi death camps and grounded in his own training as a psychotherapist. This book, *Man's*

Search for Meaning, helped put into context the varied responses to the harsh injustices and cruelties he saw and experienced firsthand during his time in Auschwitz. It describes the responses of those who lived through this horrific experience and attempts to put into context the lives of those who survived and were released. Frankl concluded that those prisoners who could find meaning in their suffering were more likely to survive the unjust acts of cruelty than those who were not able to put their suffering into some kind of meaningful context. "In accepting this challenge to suffer bravely, life has a meaning up to the last moment, and it retains the meaning literally to the end. In other words, life's meaning is an unconditional one, for it even includes the potential meaning of unavoidable suffering."[3] He wrote, "Suffering had become a task on which we did not want to turn our backs. We had realized its hidden opportunities for achievement. . . . There was plenty of suffering for us to get through."[4] First Peter seems to be saying something similar to those who would read this letter.

Next the writer addresses wives. "Wives, likewise submit to your own husbands. Do this so that even if some of them refuse to believe the word, they may be won without a word by their wives' way of life" (3:1). The debate about the meaning of this particular text still rages, and there seems to be no middle ground. For some Christians this means that the man is head of the household, just like in the days of the Roman Empire, and that is that. For other Christians this counsel represents the fossilized remains of an ancient custom that needs to be rejected by modern couples.

Much of what First Peter says about subordination of wives to their husbands does seem to be a replication of the values of the surrounding culture. Then the writer adds this twist: "Husbands, likewise, submit by living with your wife in ways that honor her, knowing that she is the weaker partner. Honor her all the more, as she is also a co-heir of the gracious care of life" (3:7). This admonition for the husband to "submit" seems to be a radical departure from the values of the Empire as they relate to family structure. For the husband to recognize his wife's place in society as the "weaker partner" is to acknowledge the reality of her position as defined by the power structure of the family. It is one thing to call people who are in a weaker position within a social structure to submit to those in a higher position. It is a quite different thing to call for those in a higher position (the husband) to submit and honor one who is in a weaker position (the wife). To describe the weaker partner as a "co-heir" is to overturn the power structure of the culture, albeit in a subtle and cautious fashion.

Finished With Sin

"Therefore, since Christ suffered as a human, you should also arm yourselves with his way of thinking. This is because whoever suffers is finished with sin" (4:1). To embrace a life of suffering love is to reject the ethics and customs of the surrounding culture. "You have wasted enough time doing what unbelievers desire" (4:3). There follows a list of immoral acts that the followers of Jesus have turned away from and acknowledgment that having done so will only gain them the scorn of their pagan neighbors. The first sign that those reading this letter are finished with sin is that they reject the standards of society in order to embrace a way of life in which even a husband may submit and honor his wife.

The second indication that those who follow Jesus are finished with sin is the example of the way they treat each other. "The end of everything has come. Therefore, be self-controlled and clearheaded so you can pray. Above all, show sincere love to each other, because love brings about the forgiveness of many sins" (4:7-8). Those who are finished with sin, who have turned away from the values of the world, have everyone to love and nothing to fear.

All this is made possible by the example that Jesus set for his followers. Suffering has become a badge of honor rather than a mark of shame. "If you are mocked because of Christ's name, you are blessed, for the Spirit of glory—indeed, the Spirit of God—rests on you" (4:14). Perhaps those who want our society to accommodate Christian practices more fully would do well to remember this counsel. We should not expect the world to accommodate us. Rather we, by our suffering love, should live as examples to the world of God's own love.

The letter ends with this blessing: "After you have suffered for a little while, the God of all grace, the one who called you into his eternal glory in Christ Jesus, will himself restore, empower, strengthen, and establish you. To him be power forever and always. Amen" (5:10-11).

Living the Story

For Christians the model of suffering love has been, is, and will always be the example of Jesus Christ. Perhaps no Christian tradition has taken the concept of suffering love as seriously as the Anabaptists, the Amish and Mennonites. In their book of martyrs is a story about the demands of following Jesus if we follow the way of suffering. In the sixteenth century when the Spanish ruled over the Netherlands, Dirk Willems was arrested and convicted of holding the wrong religious beliefs. Though he was a Christian, he was an Anabaptist, and the punishment for that crime was death. He was held captive in a castle that had been turned into a prison. One day Dirk was able to escape his cell by climbing out a window and running across the frozen moat. He had lost so much weight during his captivity that he wasn't heavy enough to break through the ice. A guard noticed that Dirk was trying to escape and followed. The guard was considerably heavier than Dirk and the ice broke beneath his feet. The guard, drowning, called for help.

Under the circumstances Dirk could have escaped easily, but his faith, the very faith that was the reason for his arrest and death sentence said that he was to follow Jesus' instruction to love his enemies. So Dirk turned around and helped the guard out of the water, saving his life. In a perfect world perhaps the guard would have let Dirk go out of gratitude, but as we all know this world is far from perfect. The guard placed Dirk under arrest a second time and he was taken back to prison and later burned at the stake.

First Peter understands the risks of accepting the way of suffering love. The Amish still have a reputation for reaching out to and loving those who wish them or do them harm. How do the rest of us who claim to be Christians embrace the suffering love that Jesus taught and lived? How do we, who are used to having others submit to us, learn to submit to others by choice simply by following the way of Jesus?

1. Wayne Meeks, *The First Urban Christians: The Social World of the Apostle Paul* (New Haven: Yale University Press, 1983), p. 30.
2. John E. Stambaugh and David L. Balch, eds. *The New Testament in Its Social Environment* (Philadelphia: The Westminster Press, 1986), p. 123.
3. Viktor E. Frankl, *Man's Search for Meaning* (New York: Pocket Books, 1985), p. 137.
4. Ibid., pp. 99-100

5.

Awaiting the End of the World

2 Peter 1:1–3:18

Claim Your Story

In the fall of 1978 I was in the middle of my second year of graduate study at Northwestern University. I spent the evening of November 18 of that year peering into the screen of a 13-inch, black and white television that graced the tiny apartment in which I lived. While my week was taken up with study, I reserved Saturday night for some stay-at-home, inexpensive entertainment. After watching the local news at 10 p.m., I tuned into *Saturday Night Live*, which was only in its second season. As I lay on the couch chuckling at the various sketches performed by an extraordinarily talented group of improvisers, I fell asleep.

When I awoke, a bit groggy from my nap, there was a sketch on the television about a religious cult in Guyana that had killed a Congressman who had come to investigate human rights abuses. Over 900 cult members had drunk poisoned Kool-aid at the direction of their leader, a radical preacher named Jim Jones. I thought to myself, "This is sick, even for *Saturday Night Live*." It was only a few minutes later, after my stupor had lifted, that the horrifying truth pierced my consciousness—this was not a sketch; this was a news report. I had slept through the end of *SNL*, and this was a special broadcast about a catastrophic event brought about by a very charismatic preacher who apparently held the power of life and death over his followers.

Now, when I read about false prophets, the first name that comes to my mind is Jim Jones. How could one man exert so much influence that people would give their children poisoned Kool-aid? Why would anyone give another person that much power over their life? These questions still haunt me. Since that time, every few years we hear about another group who had given over their free will to a charismatic individual only to meet destruction in the end.

To whom do we offer our deepest loyalty? Are we followers of a charismatic preacher, a persuasive ideology, a political party, a nation, or a denomination? Who deserves our primary allegiance? There is only one answer for Second Peter—the God who is revealed in Jesus Christ.

Enter the Bible Story

Let the Listener Beware

You will never go broke predicting the end of the world. Writers never seem to tire of writing about it, and the reading public never seems to grow weary of making writers rich who do. It seems that there will always (is that a contradiction in terms?) be an audience interested in reading about and sometimes even devoting their lives to a timeline that will end all time as we know it. This is as true today as it was two thousand years ago.

Perhaps that is why the fascination of churchgoers with the apocalyptic visions of the books of Daniel and Revelation never seems to diminish. Each year Bible studies, videos and DVDs, novels, as well as television and radio preachers arrive to tell us, once again, that the end is just around the corner. Second Peter is not intended to be just another letter about "the end of the world." Alas, it contains no timeline of events by which you can know the day and the hour of the culmination of history. I realize that these omissions will be a great disappointment to some readers.

Some teachers in the ancient world took advantage of those who expected the end of the world and were left bewildered when it did not come. When the last of those people who had known Jesus in the flesh died, it created something of a crisis for those who continued to be followers of Jesus. If the end had not come by now, was it going to come at all? Some false teachers said that the day of the Lord would never come, so live any way you want. Some took advantage of the flock they were supposed to protect. Scandals related to the misbehavior of pastors and other church leaders, usually financial or sexual misbehavior, are nothing new.

It wasn't even new when this letter was written. Second Peter suggests that the false teachers who trouble the faithful are no different from the false prophets of past time. The true mark of false teachers is their immoral behavior that is unrestrained by any ethical qualms or sense of accountability. They tell lies in order to take advantage of the followers of Jesus, and they are driven by greed (2 Peter 2:2-3). They say that, because the day of the Lord has not come, any sort of behavior is not only possible, but acceptable. Second Peter intends to reveal these teachings for the lies that they are. Yes, followers of Jesus are to be busy during this delay in the Lord's coming, but they are to be spending their time maturing in their

---

About the Christian Faith

Four Kinds of Monks

Turning again to Saint Benedict, in his Rule he describes four kinds of monks. The first are *cenobites*. These are monks who live in a community and according to a rule. They are accountable to their community and look to others for guidance and support. There are *hermits*. Hermits are monks who have years of experience living in community and are ready to live a solitary life. They have been *cenobites*, and they are still related to the community, though they live alone in a hermitage. Then there are *sarabaites*. These are monks who want to live by their own rules and no other. Their rule is whatever pleases them, and they disdain the idea of accountability to anyone. Whatever they like they consider good and holy, and whatever they don't like they call unholy. Finally there are the *gyrovagues*. These monks travel around taking advantage of the hospitality of others. They stay a few days here and a few days there with no commitment to any one community. They are simply out to get what they can from a given community, without contributing anything to its life, then move on.

The last two types of monk seem to have a lot in common with the false teachers about which Second Peter warns us. There are those who build up and contribute to the community, and there are those who simply want to take from the community and exploit its members while leading them astray by both word and example.

faith and moral development, not casting it aside. We are to fill our time with life-giving activities rather than follow the false teachers into life-destroying behavior.

The key understanding that undergirds this entire warning against being led astray is that, no matter how unfaithful and untrustworthy the false teachers may be, God is faithful and trustworthy. Don't be distracted by the cravings of the flesh or by those who would tell you that God has forgotten you. Just as in the days of Noah, God will come to rescue those who keep the faith. You see, "the Lord knows how to rescue the godly from their trials and how to keep the unrighteous for punishment on the Judgment Day" (2:9).

This letter takes seriously Jesus' teaching that no individual (that includes you and me and all those writers who claim to) knows the day or the hour that God will bring this long and convoluted narrative we call human history to a close. That doesn't mean, however, that it will never come. Perhaps this is why the stories of Jesus seem to be directed toward helping his followers live in the meantime, these meantimes, the in-between times, when the reign of God is present in seed form, planted in the soil of this ruined garden, and taking root and sprouting in the most unlikely of places.

Second Peter summarized what we are to do in the meantime at the very beginning of the letter: "This is why you must make every effort to add moral excellence to your faith; and to moral excellence, knowledge; and to knowledge, self-control; and to self-control, endurance; and to endurance, godliness; and to godliness, affection for others; and to affection for others, love" (1:5-7). Such are the attitudes and actions that the followers of Jesus are to be practicing as they await the coming of the Lord. Those who read the letter are to make this effort because, "if all these things are yours and they are growing in you, they'll keep you from becoming inactive and unfruitful in the knowledge of our Lord Jesus Christ" (1:8). Seeds of faith sown by Jesus are to be carefully cultivated so they can bear fruit.

The Patience of God

Perhaps the best known quotation from Second Peter is, "with the Lord a single day is like a thousand years and a thousand years are like a single day" (3:8). Here these words speak within the context of the delay in Jesus' return. The problem being addressed here is not predicting the Second Coming but the fact that it hasn't happened already. Some take this to mean that it will not occur . . . ever!

There is a reason that the Lord has not returned as promised. The delay is not through neglect or forgetfulness on God's part. No, it is because God wants as many people as possible to respond to the divine invitation extended in Jesus Christ to be a part of God's dream for creation. "The Lord isn't slow to keep his promise, as some think of slowness, but he is patient toward you, not wanting anyone to perish but all to change their hearts and lives" (3:9). Here Second Peter is reiterating the argument put forth by Paul in Romans 2:4 when he asks his readers if they "have contempt for God's generosity, tolerance, and patience." After two thousand years of waiting we read the words in a somewhat different context. It would be very easy for us to believe that the coming of the Lord is never going to come. Some followers of Jesus today respond by interpreting prophecies in Scripture to be a roadmap for the times we are living through. They read these prophetic words and find in them a formula by means of which to calculate the day and time of the Lord's coming. Others dismiss the Second Coming as the reflecting of some misguided ancient hope that will never come to be. In taking these stances do both of these groups demonstrate contempt for "God's generosity, tolerance, and patience"?

The one thing we can count on is that "the day of the Lord will come like a thief" (2 Peter 3:10). Here the writer picks up the language of 1 Thessalonians 5:1-2: "We don't need to write you about the timing and dates, brothers and sisters. You know very well that the day of the Lord is going to come like a thief in the night." Both draw upon the imagery that Jesus employs to emphasize that "nobody knows when that day or hour will come, not the heavenly angels and not the Son. Only the Father knows" (Matthew 24:36). Jesus adds this admonition: "Therefore, stay alert! You don't know what day the Lord is coming. But you understand that if the head of the house knew at what time the thief would come, he would keep alert and wouldn't allow the thief to break into his house" (24:42-43; also see Luke 12:39-40). If, indeed, the day of the Lord will come like a thief in the night, then our job is not to predict its coming nor are we to ignore or deny its coming. Instead, we are to stay alert and simply be involved in doing what God wants us to do.

When it comes to what we are to do while awaiting the day of the Lord, Second Peter makes this proposal: "Therefore, dear friends, while you are waiting for these things to happen, make every effort to be found by him in peace—pure and faultless" (2 Peter 3:14). The fact that we have been given this extra time is not a reason for distress but a time during which we can appreciate God's patience as a gift for the whole of humankind. "Consider the patience of the Lord to be salvation" (3:15).

These words address communities that are trying to be faithful as they make it through the meantimes, times of oppression and persecution. Second Peter offers encouragement to those who would tend the seedlings of faith that had sprouted all over the Empire from Jesus' teaching and preaching about the reign of God. Such tender plants are too easily destroyed by a hostile environment, too little or too much rain or sun. Or they are in danger of being trampled underfoot by those who are obsessed by misguided and false views of the Lord's delay and thus feel free to live greedy, dishonest, and immoral lives.

On a personal note: I was born while my parents were living at my mother's family homeplace in a very rural part of Middle Tennessee. Under ordinary circumstances I would have been born in the same farmhouse in which my grandmother had given birth to my mother thirty-three years before. Instead, because my very presence in her body had become a threat to my mother's life, we traveled to a hospital in Murray, Kentucky, for the delivery. Returning to my mother's homeplace from the hospital involved traveling paved roads, then gravel roads, and then a dirt road that at long last climbed the hill to the house. My father would tease my mother that after the dirt road ended we had to follow a horse trail, then a cow path, then a pig path until we came to the chicken yard. Only then would we know that we were home. It was common to speak of the isolated homesteads like that of my family as sitting at the end of the world, to which we answered, "It's not the end of the world, but you can see it from here."

Some preachers and commentators on apocalyptic literature even today will tell you that writings of the New Testament outline a predictable and clearly delineated pathway moving toward the end of the world. They (and only they) can tell you where the edge of time lies and, like those who believe in a flat earth, can point without hesitation or doubt to the "jumping off place." Others will say that waiting and watching for a time when God will set all things right is simply a waste of time.

Still, for more than two thousand years that horizon called the day of the Lord has kept moving. The world as we know it has not come to an end. The seeds of faith have kept sprouting across the earth and have been cultivated into communities, some planted in nurturing environments and some in decidedly hostile places. Followers of Jesus have simply continued to do those things he told his followers to do in the meantime, even the meanest of times. We do not give up, because we trust in God's patience and that what Jesus has told his followers is both trustworthy and sufficient to see us through.

I would suggest that this continuously moving horizon is a gift that allows followers of Jesus to continue to live in faith and trust, without the certainty of a future that can be predicted or controlled. In short, it is our very trust in God that allows us to continue to practice the disciplines that Jesus taught us without the need for certainty or control. So the next time we hear some preacher or writer say that they can point to a definite, predictable end of the world, just tell them, "Oh, it's not the end of the world, but you can see it from here," then return to tending the seedlings of faith that God has left in our care.

Live the Story

When I first arrive as the newly appointed pastor of a congregation, it is not unusual for someone to ask me, "What is your vision for this church?" I have to answer them honestly that I have no vision for the church at which I have just arrived. In fact, it would be presumptuous, if not downright arrogant, for me to suggest that I have come with a vision for a church whose membership and history I don't know. So what I tell them is that God has a vision and a mission for this church and my job is to help the congregation discern that vision and mission, if they have not already. If the congregation has discerned God's vision and mission for them, then my job is to hold our feet to the fire to make sure we are doing what God has called us to do.

God's vision and mission for a congregation and God's calling for each of us as individuals define our job as followers of Jesus as we wait for the day of the Lord. Our job is to stay awake and be found doing what we are called to do, not to figure out what the date of that coming might be. As an individual this is named our *vocation*, which comes from the Latin word *vocare*, which means to call. Our calling usually has to do with a way of life or an avenue of service. Our calling may or may not be related to our training or the way we earn our living. Or perhaps our calling is the way we treat people as we earn our living. In any case, our vocation is lived out in the way we spend our time doing what God wants us to do. What is your vocation?

The same is true for congregations. God's vision and mission for a congregation indicates our understanding of how we believe God expects us to apply our gifts and energy until the Lord comes to straighten everything out. Does your congregation have a vision and a mission statement? Does the congregation lift it up and try to live by it? How do you personally participate in God's vision and mission for your congregation?

6.

Living in the Light

1 John 1:1–3:24

Claim Your Story

The church I serve presently has a series of strikingly beautiful stained-glass windows on every wall of the sanctuary. In the late afternoon when the sanctuary is almost dark but the light still enters through the stained-glass windows, they create for me a very prayerful space. For many people the stained-glass windows are simply works of art, a means of decorating the neo-gothic architecture of the church and adding color to our worship space. But it was not always so. In the medieval period, when many cathedrals were built, these images made from colored glass served another, very important purpose. For a population, many of whom could not read the Scriptures, these images of color and light told the stories of their ancestors in faith. Some of these were biblical figures drawn from both Old and New Testaments. Some represented followers of Jesus whom the church has chosen to call saints. Sometimes those figures were ordinary people going about their lives, simply doing their everyday tasks.

On a trip to lecture at a theological seminary some years ago I attended worship in one of the local churches in town. Four of the stained-glass windows in that sanctuary portrayed the Gospel writers: Matthew, Mark, Luke, and John. Each was holding a book and quill, and each one was portrayed as if he was listening to a voice that I could not hear and a speaker I could not see. These windows depicted not only an artist's rendering of the Gospel writers, but also portrayed in colored glass that church's understanding of the inspiration of Scripture, at least as it was when the windows were created.

Stained-glass windows can still tell our story in a century when there are dozens of translations of the Bible available in bookstores, online, and even on e-book readers and smartphones. I was told a story by another pastor of a children's time when she was attempting to tell the children about the saints. When she asked if anyone knew what a saint was, one little girl pointed to the stained-glass windows and said, "They're the people that the light shines through." That may be the best definition of a saint I have ever heard, and one that fits very well the description of the goal of every follower of Jesus as they are described in First John. We are all called to strive to be the people the light of God shines through.

Enter the Bible Story

Living the Light

The First Letter of John does not begin like a letter at all. There are none of the niceties that one would expect like a greeting or salutation. No, the writer plunges right in to something that resembles a public announcement. As we listen to the words we can easily imagine them being spoken through a megaphone or sound system. The writer is telling us something that has been experienced directly, not given secondhand. Listen for all the action words the writer uses to describe the message:

> We **announce** to you what existed from the beginning, what we have **heard**, what we have **seen** with our own eyes, what we have **seen** and our hands **handled**, about the word of life. The life was **revealed**, and we have **seen**, and we **testify** and **announce** to you the eternal life that was with the Father and was **revealed** to us. What we have **seen** and **heard**, we also **announce** it to you so that you can have fellowship with us. Our fellowship is with the Father and with his Son, Jesus Christ. We are writing these things so that our joy can be complete. (1:1-4, **my emphasis**)

What the writer announces with such force and urgency is knowledge that has come through direct experience. And what has the writer come to know that is of such importance to communicate? "This is the message we have heard from him and announce to you: 'God is light and there is no darkness in him at all'" (1:5). Then later, "but if we live in the light in the same way as he is in the light, we have fellowship with each other, and the blood of Jesus, his Son, cleanses us from every sin" (1:7).

The first thing that First John emphasizes is the calling of each person who would claim to follow Jesus to live in the light, to live in God's light as it is revealed in Jesus Christ. The problem arises in that it is so difficult for human beings to avoid sin. Since sin is a reality in each life, we have to choose how to deal with it. There are two primary ways that we choose to deal with our sin. We either deny it (that we have committed a sin or that our actions were truly sinful) or we can confess our sin. The strategy that seems to come most naturally to humans is the route of denial. First John addresses this human tendency with stern words: "If we claim, 'We don't have any sin,' we deceive ourselves and the truth is not in us. But if we confess our sins, he is faithful and just to forgive us our sins and cleanse us from everything we've done wrong. If we claim, 'We have never sinned,' we make him a liar and his word is not in us" (1:8-10).

Perhaps the first step in acknowledging our sin is to admit that we are not the source of the light. God is the source of the light. We are simply to live in that light in such a way that others can see the light of God reflected in our lives. The good news is that we don't have to be sinless to reflect God's light. In fact, the admission that we do sin, the honesty and authenticity it takes to say so, clears the way for us to become people who reflect the light.

Our recognition of our sinfulness is not a hindrance because we are not the source of light. The fire is the source of the light, but we are not the fire. Just as the moon reflects the light of the sun but does not produce its own light, the light we are to reflect is not our own but light from God. How, then, do we reflect the light of God? For First John the answer is simple. We follow the example of Jesus: "The one who claims to remain in him [Jesus Christ] ought to live in the same way as he lived" (2:6).

This is nothing new according to First John: "Dear friends, I am not writing a new commandment to you, but an old commandment that you had from the beginning" (1 John 2:7). The idea that God is the source of

About the Scripture

Light Shines in Darkness

In modern times it is easy to forget what darkness is really like. We are surrounded by street lights and headlights, by incandescent lights and fluorescent lights, the lights of nearby cities and the lights of nearby televisions. Unless we find ourselves at a retreat center in the woods or at a camp in the desert far from artificial sources of light, we can forget how dark it gets at night, especially when the moon and stars are hidden by clouds. Because we can flip on a light switch in any room in our house or depend on the light that shines in the window, even at night we might not have any idea how dark the houses in the ancient world were, even in the daytime.

In the time in which this letter was written, all light except that of the sun depended on fire; usually the flame of an oil lamp provided illumination inside. Outside, torches would be lighted in order to light the way for travel at night. Fire had to be carefully cultivated and protected. If your fire went out, there was no cooking nor heat nor light. Fire had to be carried from place to place or borrowed from a neighbor. In some cases flint could be used to set dry grass or shavings ablaze in order to start a flame again. When the night was dark, and they were often very dark, one had to have fire in order to have light.

Jesus told his followers: "You are the light of the world. A city on top of a hill can't be hidden. Neither do people light a lamp and put it under a basket. Instead, they put it on top of a lampstand, and it shines on all who are in the house. In the same way, let your light shine before people, so they can see the good things you do and praise your Father who is in heaven" (Matthew 5:14-16). According to Jesus, "the good things we do" constitute the light that must not be hidden. Is Jesus counseling his followers to make a show of their goodness in order to draw attention to themselves? No, a light is not placed on a lampstand for people to stare at the flame emerging from the tip of the lamp. Rather, a light on a lampstand is there so one can see how to move about the room. The light we reflect is for the sake of others—a city on a hill to show the traveler the way and a lamp on a stand so others can find their way around the dark room.

light and that we are to reflect that light can be traced back to the first words spoken at creation, when God spoke light into the darkness. Then the writer makes an abrupt turnabout and seems to offer a contradictory message. "On the other hand, I am writing a new commandment to you, which is true in him and in you, because the darkness is passing away and the true light already shines" (2:8).

There is one true test that this new/old commandment is being followed: "The one who claims to be in the light while hating a brother or sister is in the darkness even now. The person loving a brother and sister stays in the light, and there is nothing in the light that causes a person to stumble. But the person who hates a brother or sister is in the darkness and lives in the darkness, and doesn't know where to go because the darkness blinds the eyes" (2:9-11). To live in the light is to reflect God's love. To hate (refuse to reflect God's love) is to walk in darkness; and as we all know, those who walk in darkness are most likely to stumble.

Choosing the Good

Everyone who lives is confronted with choices. For the readers of First John the choices are even more urgent because, the writer asserts, "It is the last hour" (2:18). We are enabled to make the loving choices because our lives are grounded in a relationship with Jesus. We did not, however, initiate this relationship—God did. "See what kind of love the Father has given to us in that we should be called God's children, and that is what we are!" (3:1). This gift from God is not a static state that a believer inhabits, but is a dynamic relationship into which the follower of Jesus grows. "Dear friends, now we are God's children, and it hasn't yet appeared what we will be. We know that when he appears we will be like him because we'll see him as he is" (3:2). We are not only to follow the example of Jesus; we are to grow into the image of the risen Christ. This, too, is God's gift.

This does not mean that the follower of Jesus has no part in the process of growing into his image. When we choose the good, the loving way, we participate in the transformation that God is working in and through us. "Little children, make sure that no one deceives you. The person who practices righteousness is righteous, in the same way that Jesus is righteous" (3:7). On the other hand, we have the freedom to choose the sinful, or hateful, way. "The person who practices sin belongs to the devil, because the devil has been sinning since the beginning. God's Son appeared for this purpose: to destroy the works of the devil" (3:8). Notice that the writer does not say that Jesus came to destroy people who sin, or even the devil, but "the works of the devil."

First John makes the connection among living the light, righteousness, and love explicit: "Everyone who doesn't practice righteousness is not from God, including the person who doesn't love a brother or sister. This is the message that you heard from the beginning: love one another" (3:10-11). Here the writer reiterates the new/old message, the "message that you heard from the beginning," to choose the good is to make the loving choice toward another.

To this the writer adds another layer. Here we are not only talking about light/darkness, righteousness/sin, and love/hate. First John adds to these the choice between life and death. "We know that we have transferred from death to life, because we love the brothers and sisters. The person who does not love remains in death" (3:14). According to the writer of this letter the means by which we are transferred from life to death is exactly the same as that which allows us to move from darkness to light, from sin to righteousness, and from hatred to love—following the example set for us by Jesus. "This is how we know love: Jesus laid down his life for us, and we ought to lay down our lives for our brothers and sisters" (3:16).

While all these transformations are a gift from God, this does not mean that our participation is passive. We need to be aware of the things that can get in the way of our love for our brothers and sisters. It probably was an indictment of the behavior of certain Christians of that time, and certainly may indict some Christians today, that the writer feels the need to add this caution: "But if a person has material possessions and sees a brother or sister in need and that person doesn't care—how can the love of God remain in him?" (3:17). It doesn't really matter how we feel about the person in need or how that person came to be in those circumstances. Rather, it is the love of God working through us that allows us to reach out no matter how we feel. After all, love is not just a feeling; it is a way of living and treating others.

A second, and somewhat surprising, thing that can stand in our way is self-condemnation. This is a helpful word for Christians today as well as those persons to whom First John is addressed. "Even if our hearts condemn us, God is greater than our hearts and knows all things. Dear friends, if our hearts don't condemn us, we have confidence in relationship to God" (3:20-21). Self-condemnation is self-defeating. Confidence in God takes away self-condemnation so that we are freed to grow into the likeness of God's love in Jesus Christ.

Followers of Jesus are not simply to talk about the light and righteous and love. No, we are called to be active participants in God's light, love, and righteousness. "Little children, let's not love with words or speech but with action and truth" (3:18). This echoes James's emphasis on doing the truth, acting in love, getting out on the field and into the mix of life, and not just talking a good game. The writer sums up this portion of the letter by restating the new/old commandment in a little different way: "This is his commandment, that we believe in the name of his Son, Jesus Christ, and love each other as he commanded us" (3:23). So, belief cannot be separated from action. If we say we believe one thing but act in a way that contradicts that belief—we are lying to ourselves, to others, and to God. "The person who keeps his commandments [to love each other] remains in God and God remains in him; and this is how we know that he remains in us, because of the Spirit that he has given to us" (3:24). The next section of the letter helps the readers know just how to recognize God's Spirit at work in their lives.

Living the Story

When I was a youngster I was, first, a Cub Scout, then a Boy Scout. Though I never made it past the Second Class rank as a Boy Scout, I learned certain lessons during that time that have stayed with me. The Scout Law for example: "A Scout is trustworthy, loyal, helpful, friendly, courteous, kind, obedient, cheerful, thrifty, brave, clean, and reverent." (Believe it or not I typed this from memory!) An unwritten rule, though a powerful influence on scouts of my era, was the idea that we would do *at least* one good deed each day. We were not limited to one good deed, but we were expected to be on the lookout at all times for the chance so that we didn't go an entire day without helping someone in a substantial way.

First John seems to operate on a similar set of expectations. Followers of Jesus are to live in the light by choosing the good. Choosing the good involves an active participation in loving rather than hating. To live in the light of God's love involves sharing that light. This involves an active participation on the part of Christians in the activity of God already taking place in the world around us. We are to reflect the light not so much in the blissful smiles on our faces, but in the ways that we are constantly on the lookout for opportunities to do good for others.

What would happen if we in our church were pledged to look for ways to reflect God's light and love by the good we do for others, especially those less fortunate? With God's help we are able to move beyond the love of material possessions and self-condemnation that stand in our way. Because God has taken the initiative to call us beloved children, we are activated to reach out to others as beloved children, our brothers and sisters. This would not only transform our lives as Christians, I think, but would also make a huge difference in our congregations and in the communities around them.

How are you and your congregation living out the new/old commandment to love? How is the light of God shining through you?

7.

Love Is a Policy

1 John 4:1–3 John 15

Claim Your Story

Relationships between groups of people of different races or ethnic backgrounds or cultures or who speak different languages have always been complicated. Often, we mistrust those who are different from us. We use that mistrust as a reason to exclude them or hate them or even kill them. Sadly enough, this is frequently true of people who claim the name of Christian.

But sometimes, amazingly, relationships take a different turn, have a different character. Have you ever observed or been a part of a situation in which Christian love overcame hatred? How did that happen? What made that possible?

Some years ago a United Methodist pastor friend of mine, Bill, worked in an Urban Ministries Center in a large city in the South. Though he was white he became good friends with an African American woman named Mary. They had both grown up in the segregated South with its separate bathrooms and water fountains for "White" and "Colored," its fire bombings of houses and churches, and its lynchings. They might as well have grown up on two different planets, although in the same galaxy.

After a number of years working together serving those who were less fortunate, their friendship grew to the point that they could talk about almost anything. One day in the midst of a conversation, Bill broached a topic that he had wondered about for some time. "We grew up in the same city, but we might as well have been from different continents. You and I went to different schools and used different public facilities. I know that your people were excluded from lunch counters and movie theaters. I know some of the names that white people called you just because of the color of your skin. I read about your neighbors who were harassed and your churches that were fire bombed. Given the history of the relationship between our people, I can't figure out why you don't hate me."

After a brief pause Mary replied, "You know, Bill, if it wasn't for Jesus, I would." If the love of Christ does not fill us, if the light of God's love doesn't shine through us, we easily fall into the patterns that our culture or ethnic background or race or national heritage says is acceptable. If it wasn't for Jesus we could exclude and hate and even kill others because of their differences. On the other hand if we see others as brothers and sisters in Christ such actions are not an option. You see, those who abide in love abide in God and God abides in them.

Enter the Bible Story

Chapter 3 of First John ended with the claim that God's Spirit had been given to the readers of this letter. This is the evidence that God remains in us and that we remain in God. The very next line, though, suggests that not every spirit is a gift from God and that the followers of Jesus have to be careful which spirit work they participate in.

Many people today would say that they are spiritual but not religious. Lots of Christians are quick to take issue with this description, because they see it as a means of avoiding the responsibilities of religious life, especially Christian life. At some level the writer of First John would agree: "This is how you know if a spirit comes from God: every spirit that confesses that Jesus Christ has come as a human is from God, and every spirit that doesn't confess Jesus is not from God" (1 John 4:2-3). The idea that Jesus has become human as well as divine is central to First John. To profess belief in Jesus is not simply to say "I believe," as we learned in the first three chapters of First John. To confess that Jesus Christ has become human is to act as if God's love has, indeed, been born and walks among us in the flesh, then to follow that example.

The true test of the spirits as well as the true test of what we believe can be summed up in one word: *agápē*, the Greek word that the writer of First John uses for love. Our love is to be like God's love, a generous-hearted, self-giving love that lives out the words of Jesus as quoted by Paul: "It is more blessed to give than to receive" (Acts 20:35).

The standard against which the spirits as well as our belief and our practice is to be measured is *agápē*. "Dear friends, let's love each other, because love is from God, and everyone who loves is born from God and knows God. The person who doesn't love does not know God, because God is love" (1 John 4:7-8).

God's Love Comes First

First John asserts that we can love because we have been loved. God loved us first, before we even were aware that we wanted or needed to be loved, and certainly before we could love anyone in return. In short, God loved us before we could love God back. "Dear friends, if God loved us this way, we also ought to love each other. No one has ever seen God. If we love each other, God remains in us and his love is made perfect in us" (4:11-12). When we love each other, this writer suggests, we show God to the person we love and to others who observe that love. In short, love is the primary and most profound witness to faith in God

Then First John makes an even more radical statement about the nature of this *agápē*, the same sacrificial love that God showed the world in Jesus Christ, that we are supposed to share with others. Not only do we show forth God's love in our lives, we abide in God and God abides in us. To abide is not to simply pay a short visit. To abide is to remain, to be in a relationship for the long haul. First John states it clearly: "God is love, and those who remain in love remain in God and God remains in them. This is how love has been perfected in us, so that we can have confidence on the Judgment Day, because we are exactly the same as God in this world" (4:16-17). **Exactly the same as God in this world!!!** What is that supposed to mean? Well, it doesn't mean that we are to consider ourselves gods, nor does it even mean that we are perfect people.

One of John Wesley's most controversial ideas was that people could be made perfect in love in this life. There was a lot of confusion around the idea of "going on to perfection" in his time and there still is today. By suggesting that we could be made perfect in love, he suggested that, for the most part, this process was not our doing, but a gift from God. We simply participate in God's gift. In addition, he didn't mean that someone who was perfected in love was mistake-less and would never sin again. That's not what Mr. Wesley seems to mean by perfection. Rather, to be made perfect in love simply means that we participate in God's gift of love for this world to the extent that we love as God loves. That is exactly what the writer of First John seems to be telling us here. Being perfected in love is not something for which we can take credit but is a process in which we can take part. We simply pass along the love of God that has been poured out so generously upon us; we reflect the love of God that has first shone upon us.

While such love does not protect us from making mistakes, it does have a very positive side effect. "There is no fear in love, but perfect love drives out fear, because fear expects punishment. The person who is afraid has not been made perfect in love" (4:18). Jesus seems to be fearless. When a crowd wanted to throw him off the edge of a hill after he preached, he calmly walked through the crowd. In the midst of a storm on the Sea of Galilee, he instructs the storm to calm down. Jesus' quiet strength and fearlessness is evident in the presence of Pilate, who has the power to put

About the Christian Faith

Prevenient Grace

Prevenient grace is the term John Wesley, and now many others, have used to describe God's love for us that precedes our knowledge of God or love or pretty much anything else. Just as parents love a child before that child has done anything to earn or deserve that love, so God loves us without our having done anything to justify that love. God does not love us because of what we have done or not done, or because of who we are. God loves us because of who God is. "We love because God first loved us" (1 John 4:19).

him to death. When we learn to love as God loves, it simply leaves everything and everyone to love and nothing and no one to fear or to hate.

Not only is fear gone from our hearts; there is no reason to hate another as well. In fact, if we continue to hate after God has loved us so freely and undeservedly, we deny the very love we say we have for God. "We love because God first loved us. If anyone says, I love God, and hates a brother or sister, he is a liar, because the person who doesn't love a brother or sister who can be seen can't love God, who can't be seen. This commandment we have from him: those who love God ought to love their brother and sister also" (4:19-21).

These are strong words, but Jesus takes it one step further: "You have heard that it was said, You must love your neighbor and hate your enemy. But I say to you, love your enemies and pray for those who harass you so that you will be acting as children of your Father who is in heaven. He makes the sun rise on both the evil and the good and sends rain on both the righteous and the unrighteous. If you love only those who love you, what reward do you have? Don't even the tax collectors do the same? And if you greet only your brothers and sisters, what more are you doing? Don't even the Gentiles do the same? Therefore, just as your heavenly Father is complete in showing love to everyone, so also you must be complete" (Matthew 5:43-48).

Reminder Notes

I have come to the age that I have to write reminder notes for myself and put them in conspicuous places so I will notice them. Often these are written on sticky notes that I put on the refrigerator or the door frame through which I exit to go to the car. Though we are not sure that the same person wrote all three letters, Second John and Third John are reminder notes about some of the issues that were examined at greater length in First John.

Both Second John and Third John begin in the traditional fashion of ancient letters, unlike First John, which has none of the typical mechanisms for beginning a letter. Besides, First John is directed to a community, while Second John and Third John are directed to individuals. Both let-

About the Scripture

Three Words for Love

Whereas in English we have one primary word for love, in Greek there are several. The Greek word *érōs* refers to that love that emerges from desire or need. In English we get our word *erotic* from this Greek source. In our language, erotic typically refers to sexual desire; but in the Greek that is not necessarily the case. We might say that *érōs* is that love whose energy is directed toward one's self. While the beloved might experience that same desire or need, that is not necessarily the case.

A second word in Greek that we would translate as love is *philía*. This is the kind of love we experience with friends or family members. While there is an element of need that fuels *philía*, the difference here is that it is mutual and goes both ways. This kind of love is shared and the energy moves both toward one's self and away from one's self toward the other person. The name of the city Philadelphia comes from this Greek source and is where it gets its motto "The City of Brotherly Love."

A third Greek word that can mean love is *agápē*, which is the kind of self-giving love that we as Christians associate with God's love. It is the kind of love in which the energy flows out of one's self toward the beloved without expectation of its being returned. Some would call it unconditional love. *Agápē* is the term used in the First Letter of John when it says, "God is love, and those who remain in love remain in God and God remains in them" (1 John 4:16) and later, "There is no fear in love, but perfect love drives out fear" (4:18).

While Christians as human beings experience every type of love, it is this last type, *agápē*, that we are called upon to practice if we are to love as God loves.

---

ters are simply designated as being "From the elder" (2 John 1; 3 John 1). The name John is never mentioned in these books; and it was not until the fourth century that they were attributed to a "John the Elder," as distinct from "John the Evangelist," whose name is associated with the Fourth Gospel. It appears that the same person wrote these two letters, but not necessarily that First John was written by the same hand. In any case, they remind us of some of the core issues with which First John is concerned.

Also, these two letters are addressed to very specific people who are mentioned in the beginning of the letters, one of those being "the chosen gentlewoman and her children" and the other to "my dear friend Gaius, whom I truly love." Each of these is followed by a blessing for the recipient of the letter.

Second John contains a reminder that we are to love each other and that we are to beware of deceivers. This echoes the language and some of the concerns of First John. The Third Letter of John seems to be a more personal word of praise for Gaius's hospitality to brothers and sisters who pass his way, even though he doesn't know them. His behavior is contrasted with Diotrephes who does not extend hospitality to the brothers and sisters, because he "likes to put himself first" (3 John 9).

Both letters end with a word about why they are so brief. It is because the writer intends to see the persons to whom the letters are addressed, visit with them, and talk with them "face-to-face." It is a helpful reminder to modern readers that the New Testament Epistles were meant to be read aloud, in the case of Second John and Third John to an individual; but often they are intended to be read to a community or several communities. Even if they are read aloud, though, any letter is a poor substitute for face-to-face communication.

Live the Story

Everywhere you turn today you hear about love. Love songs populate the radio and television. There are entire cable channels devoted to movies about love. *Love* as a word is used to describe any number of human experiences. These include infatuation, lust, friendship, devotion, desire. We apply the word *love* to everything from family members and friends to boyfriends and girlfriends to husbands and wives to foods or cars.

None of these are adequate to describe the kind of love spoken of in the letters of John. For the writer, love is not a feeling. Love is not a culturally defined experience or relationship. Some years ago one of my professors told us, "Love is not a feeling. Love is a policy." Love, according to my professor, is the way we choose to treat others, no matter how we may feel about them. According to John's letters, love is our policy because, first, it is God's policy. *Agápē* is not the kind of love that depends on circumstances. *Agápē* is that kind of love that depends only on the nature of the one who does the loving.

God's love is the love that can overcome hatred, a love that is stronger than death. When we live in God's love, God lives and loves through us.

This is a love that leads to life, not death. The way others will know that God's love lives in us is that they see us love one another.

What are you doing to implement love as a policy? What more could you be doing? What more are you ready to do?

8.

Holding Fast to What Is Important

Jude

Claim Your Story

There is a folk tale in which someone on a hike in the woods gets lost. After wandering in the forest for some time and experiencing the panic that overtakes those who have lost their way, the hiker encounters an old man with a long beard and long hair. "Thank goodness," the hiker exclaims. "Do you know the way that leads out of the forest?" The old man answered, "I have been wandering the trails that meander through these woods for years, but I cannot show you the path that leads out of the forest." "What good is that?" the hiker replies, almost in despair. The old man responded, "While I may not be able to show you the path out of the woods, I can certainly steer you away from all the many paths that do not lead out of the forest."

Many people in modern society feel as if they are lost in a dense forest. For some it is a forest of dead-end jobs or no job at all. For others the forest is populated by a series of broken relationships. Others are surrounded by a forest of debt. For others there is confusion about what to believe and who to believe. Advertisers will attempt to sell us things that are supposed to help, but they rarely do. The "stuff" that we are sold may distract us from our feeling of lostness for a time, but soon this distraction loses its power and we feel as lost or more lost than ever. Have you ever felt this sense of lostness?

The Letter of Jude begins by pointing out a number of ways that do not lead out of the forest. These are solutions offered by those who would lead the followers of Jesus astray. For Jude there is a way out of the forest of the brokenness of our world and our own brokenness as human beings. If we continue to follow Jesus, without getting sidetracked by the distractions that lead us off the path, we will ultimately find the way. First, though, we have to find and reject all the paths that do not lead out of the forest.

Enter the Bible Story

The Letter of Jude begins in a fairly typical fashion by stating who the letter is from, to whom it is addressed, then following these with a brief blessing. When the writer begins to state the intention of the letter, however, things begin to get interesting. Originally the writer was going to reflect with the readers on "the salvation we share" (verse 3). Instead, something has come to the writer's attention that has required a change of plans. Both the change and the reason are revealed in the next sentences: "I must write to urge you to fight for the faith delivered once and for all to God's holy people [the new intention]. Godless people have slipped in among you. They turn the grace of our God into unrestrained immorality and deny our only master and Lord, Jesus Christ [the cause] (verses 3b-4a).

Jude is likely referring here to traveling evangelists who would move from community to community spreading the idea that, in the freedom Christ brings, his followers had been freed from all moral constraints. Their motive appears to have been to take advantage of the persons they could persuade to their point of view. Charlatans and hucksters are nothing new to Christian communities. There is never a lack of stories about preachers and evangelists who are out only for what they can get.

What are these charlatans accused of? They "pollute themselves, reject authority, and slander the angels. . . . These people slander whatever they don't understand. They are destroyed by what they know instinctively, as though they were irrational animals" (verses 8b-10). Later Jude adds, "These are faultfinding grumblers, living according to their own desires. They speak arrogant words and they show partiality to people when they want a favor in return" (verse 16). They are scoffers, "living according to their own ungodly desires," who, "create divisions" (verses 18, 19). These are clearly unpleasant folks who grumble and scoff and do whatever they desire to do no matter how ungodly the desire. Then they enjoy it when they can stir up a conflict in the community.

The attitude of these evangelists is reminiscent of any number of ad campaigns that urge, "Don't wait!" "Do it now!" "Get it now!" "You deserve it!" "You only go around once!" Today we are very familiar with the attitude, "I'll do whatever I want to do. It's a free country. It's nobody else's business." In fact, this is probably the most common interpretation of freedom to be found in modern American culture. This attitude of doing whatever I want no matter how it may affect the lives of others can be seen in behavior from the world of high finance to that of drug dealers. What does Jude have to say to a culture that encourages and thrives on the attitude that the writer finds so destructive to Christian life and faith? More importantly, what do we as Christians have to say about this "freedom" we find ourselves surrounded by today?

One indictment offered by Jude that can be easily overlooked is that these false teachers show favoritism to those who can do them a favor in return. Remember what Jesus said about that: "Then Jesus said to the person who had invited him, 'When you host a lunch or dinner, don't invite your friends, your brothers and sisters, your relatives, or rich neighbors. If you do, they will invite you in return and that will be your reward. Instead,

About the Christian Faith

Antinomianism

The people who are threatening life in the community to which Jude is writing practice a theology that came much later to be called *antinomianism*. The name comes from two Greek words, *anti* meaning against and *nomos* meaning law. The term was coined during the Protestant Reformation by Martin Luther to describe those who took his emphasis on salvation by faith alone to mean that none of the biblical laws applied to them. While the specific word, *antinomian*, is a product of the sixteenth century, the theology and behavior it describes has been around from the early days of Christianity.

when you give a banquet, invite the poor, crippled, lame, and blind. And you will be blessed because they can't repay you. Instead, you will be repaid when the just are resurrected'" (Luke 14:12-14). Doing good only for those who can do good for us, those who can repay the favor, is the road to corruption, as we can see in any number of political, financial, and governmental institutions. The common good, especially the needs of "the poor, crippled, lame, and blind" are forgotten in the rush to serve those who are already privileged because they will share their money and privileges only with those who can do them a favor in return.

Freedom, Not License

The idea that Jesus Christ had set his followers free was subject to a wide variety of interpretations as the early congregations of those followers found their way. For some it meant freedom from certain laws that had been inherited from the Jewish tradition. For example, in the Acts of the Apostles, after Saul has experienced a dramatic encounter with the risen Christ, become Paul, and taken upon himself the mission to the Gentiles, the question arose about whether these new converts had to follow all the laws of Judaism, though they were not originally Jewish. Did the men have to be circumcised and families follow the Jewish dietary laws in order to join the communities of the followers of Jesus? The discussion about these issues is recorded in Acts 15. James, the leader of the congregation in Jerusalem announces the decision: "Therefore, I conclude that we shouldn't create problems for Gentiles who turn to God. Instead, we should write a letter, telling them to avoid the pollution associated with idols, sexual immorality, eating meat from strangled animals, and consuming blood. After all, Moses has been proclaimed in every city for a long time, and is read aloud every Sabbath in every synagogue" (Acts 15:19-21).

The decision was that some of the rules inherited from the Jewish tradition apply to new converts, but not all of them. This clarification was a help, but was not without its problems. If Jewish and Gentile converts were not required to follow the same set of laws, then couldn't every ethnic group within the Gentile population follow a different set of rules?

Could not each congregation make up its own laws? Or even do away with all laws? Even after the decision at the Council of Jerusalem, there were those who went from congregation to congregation preaching that every follower of Jesus was required to follow the entirety of Jewish law including circumcision and keeping kosher. Paul had to address just such issues in his Letter to the Galatians. To those who have been influenced by such attitudes, Paul writes, "Look, I, Paul, am telling you that if you have yourselves circumcised, having Christ won't help you. Again I swear to every man who has himself circumcised that he is required to do the whole Law. You people who are trying to be made righteous by the Law have been estranged from Christ. You have fallen away from grace! We eagerly wait for the hope of righteousness through the Spirit by faith. Being circumcised or not being circumcised doesn't matter in Christ Jesus, but faith working through love does matter" (Galatians 5:2-6).

On the other hand, Paul does not want his insistence that Gentile converts don't have to follow the entirety of Jewish law to be interpreted as permission to ignore their responsibility to God and their neighbor: "You were called to freedom, brothers and sisters; only don't let this freedom be an opportunity to indulge your selfish impulses, but serve each other through love. All the Law has been fulfilled in a single statement: Love your neighbor as yourself. But if you bite and devour each other, be careful that you don't get eaten up by each other! I say be guided by the Spirit and you won't carry out your selfish desires. A person's selfish desires are set against the Spirit, and the Spirit is set against one's selfish desires. They are opposed to each other, so you shouldn't do whatever you want to do" (5:13-17).

The congregation to which the Letter of Jude is written is facing this situation. Apparently it has been infiltrated by antinomian teachers and preachers who are telling its members that none of the laws apply to them and they are free to do whatever their desires lead them to do.

Stories and Metaphors

In order to "fight for the faith," Jude chooses the rhetoric of story and metaphor. References are included to the Exodus, the destruction of

Sodom and Gomorrah, Cain, Balaam, and Korah. These stories all contain images of faithlessness and the punishment that results. These references seem to be intended as cautionary tales mentioned to give members of the congregation stories that might just help them keep their wits about them and bring those on the wrong track to their senses.

In addition to stories, Jude employs a series of metaphors to describe those who would lead the followers of Jesus astray. Each metaphor is intended to be an elaboration on the statement that introduces them: "They care only for themselves" (Jude 12). It seems that the writer here finds prose no longer sufficient to express the destruction brought about by those who feel the law doesn't apply to them. The language now changes to that of poetry. These people whose concern is only for their own welfare are:

- Waterless clouds (producing no rain)
- Fruitless trees (producing no fruit)
- Twice dead (wow, not once but twice)

About the Scripture

Allusions to Two Apocryphal Stories

There are references in Jude to two stories that may be confusing to the modern Christian reader. The first is to "the archangel Michael, when he argued with the devil about Moses' body" (verse 9). If you don't remember that story from Scripture, you're in good company. It doesn't appear anywhere in the Bible. The reference here seems to be from a text entitled "The Testament of Moses" (also called "The Assumption of Moses"), an apocryphal text that doesn't appear in either the Hebrew Bible or the New Testament.

The reference to Enoch ("who lived seven generations after Adam" [verse 14] and who was the great-grandfather of Noah) prophesying comes from another apocryphal writing entitled First Enoch. It's not in the Bible either. The Bible says of Enoch, "Enoch walked with God and disappeared because God took him" (Genesis 5:24). Enoch, who went walking with God and was no more, is one of two biblical characters in the Jewish tradition who go to God without having to pass through death. The other is Elijah.

- Uprooted (having no stability)
- Wild waves of the sea (destructive rather than creative)
- Wandering stars (aimless, for whom the darkness is not home but an underworld)

Here is my own poem, called "Eulogy for the Antinomians," which draws upon the poetry of Jude:

> Those who know no law
> Who follow their own desires without restraint
> Who care for no needs but their own
> Are pushed around by desires and needs,
> Become clouds that produce no rain.
> Bullied by the winds,
> Without rain the trees produce no fruit.
> The poor go hungry, not just for a season,
> But forever; the dead trees fall, their roots
> Reach out like the spindly fingers
> Of the starving, craving nourishment.
> On the sea the waves are wild, uncontrolled,
> The most experienced sailor cannot navigate them.
> The mouth of the deep is frothing like a hydrophobic dog.
> Above, stars wander aimlessly.
> The dark that should have been the stage
> For their one shining moment
> Has become a living hell.

So What Is a Christian to Do?

Jude offers a brief passage of instructions for the followers of Jesus in this community under siege. These can be broken down into three words of counsel on (A) How to treat each other; (B) How to treat doubters; and (C) How to treat those who have been captivated by the false teachers.

(A) How to treat each other. "But you dear friends: build each other up on the foundation of your most holy faith, pray in the Holy Spirit, keep each other in the love of God, wait for the mercy of the Lord Jesus Christ, who will give you eternal life" (verses 20-21). Listen to the verbs in this passage. When faced with an attack on our faith we are to build each other up, pray in the Spirit, keep each other in love, and wait for Jesus' mercy. This is great advice for any congregation any time. What Jude does here is to offer a brief outline of the basics about how followers of Jesus are to live together in community.

(B) How to treat doubters. "Have mercy on those who doubt. Save some by snatching them from the fire" (verses 22-23a). Notice that it does not say to chastise or condemn those who doubt. Condemnation too often pushes people away from the very God whose mercy we are trying to proclaim. It is only mercy that communicates mercy, human mercy embodying God's mercy.

(C) How to treat those who have been captivated by the false teachers. "Fearing God, have mercy on some, hating even the clothing contaminated by their sinful urges" (verse 23b). Here again Jude counsels mercy, even for those who are caught up in their sins. At first this may sound like love the sinner, hate the sin, but it is more subtle than that. Followers of Jesus are called to show mercy to anyone caught up in sin, even though we hate the destructive effects (contaminated clothing) that sinful behavior may have caused. Beginning with rebuke, Jude ends in mercy.

Live the Story

In the popular musical *Fiddler on the Roof*, Tevye sees all the traditions around which he has built his life going by the wayside. The play opens with a description of life in Anatevka the village in which Tevye has lived all his life. Life is difficult and precarious for the villagers. They are like a fiddler perched on a roof, playing their music, while at any time they could topple off. According to Tevye's spoken and sung introduction to life in Anatevka, the one thing that keeps their life from crashing to the ground is tradition. The changes that the modern word is bringing to his village are a threat to the glue of tradition that has held life together.

Though it is based on stories written by a Yiddish writer, Sholem Aleichem, in the 1890s, it is no surprise that the musical, which opened in 1964, ran for over 3,000 performances. The 1960s were a time when many people felt, like Tevye, that the traditions that had held society together were under siege. Tevye spoke aloud the fears of an entire generation of parents.

Traditions are important in families and in a culture. I remember when our daughters were young if we did something once it was an innovation, but if we did something twice it had become a tradition, especially if we did it around a holiday. The Advent calendar and candles must appear at the beginning of that season, and we had to attend a specific Christmas concert and production of *The Nutcracker*. Even as young adults our girls expect certain traditions to be observed.

The congregation to which the Letter of Jude is written is trying to hold fast to traditions that have been handed down from the apostles. Those traditions are being threatened by a group of people who interpret the freedom they have in Jesus to mean that they can do whatever they want with whomever they want whenever they want, even if it goes against those traditions.

What are some of the traditions in your family or congregation that have shaped your life and faith? How do you preserve those traditions that have positive effects? Are there any traditions that are not really helpful in growing as a disciple of Jesus? How do you let go of those?

It seems appropriate to end this study with the blessing that the writer of the Letter of Jude chose to end this letter.

> To the one who is able to protect you from falling,
> and to present you blameless and rejoicing before his
> glorious presence,
> to the only God our savior, through Jesus Christ our Lord,
> belong glory, majesty, power, and authority,
> before all time, now and forever. Amen. (verses 24-25)

Leader Guide

People often view the Bible as a maze of obscure people, places, and events from centuries ago and struggle to relate it to their daily lives. IMMERSION invites us to experience the Bible as a record of God's loving revelation to humankind. These studies recognize our emotional, spiritual, and intellectual needs and welcome us into the Bible story and into deeper faith.

As leader of an IMMERSION group, you will help participants to encounter the Word of God and the God of the Word that will lead to new creation in Christ. You do not have to be an expert to lead; in fact, you will participate with your group in listening to and applying God's life-transforming Word to your lives. You and your group will explore the building blocks of the Christian faith through key stories, people, ideas, and teachings in every book of the Bible. You will also explore the bridges and points of connection between the Old and New Testaments.

Choosing and Using the Bible

The central goal of IMMERSION is engaging the members of your group with the Bible in a way that informs their minds, forms their hearts, and transforms the way they live out their Christian faith. Participants will need this study book and a Bible. IMMERSION is an excellent accompaniment to the Common English Bible (CEB). It shares with the CEB four common aims: clarity of language, faith in the Bible's power to transform lives, the emotional expectation that people will find the love of God, and the rational expectation that people will find the knowledge of God.

Other recommended study Bibles include *The New Interpreter's Study Bible* (NRSV), *The New Oxford Annotated Study Bible* (NRSV), *The HarperCollins Study Bible* (NRSV), the *NIV and TNIV Study Bibles*, and the *Archaeological Study Bible* (NIV). Encourage participants to use more than one translation. *The Message: The Bible in Contemporary Language* is a modern paraphrase of the Bible, based on the original languages. Eugene H. Peterson has created a masterful presentation of the Scripture text, which is best used alongside rather than in place of the CEB or another primary English translation.

One of the most reliable interpreters of the Bible's meaning is the Bible itself. Invite participants first of all to allow Scripture to have its say. Pay attention to context. Ask questions of the text. Read every passage with curiosity, always seeking to answer the basic Who? What? Where? When? and Why? questions.

Bible study groups should also have handy essential reference resources in case someone wants more information or needs clarification on specific words, terms, concepts, places, or people mentioned in the Bible. A Bible dictionary, Bible atlas, concordance, and one-volume Bible commentary together make for a good, basic reference library.

The Leader's Role

An effective leader prepares ahead. This leader guide provides easy-to-follow, step-by-step suggestions for leading a group. The key task of the leader is to guide discussion and activities that will engage heart and head and will invite faith development. Discussion questions are included, and you may want to add questions posed by you or your group. Here are suggestions for helping your group engage Scripture:

State questions clearly and simply.

Ask questions that move Bible truths from "outside" (dealing with concepts, ideas, or information about a passage) to "inside" (relating to the experiences, hopes, and dreams of the participants).

Work for variety in your questions, including compare and contrast, information recall, motivation, connections, speculation, and evaluation.

Avoid questions that call for yes-or-no responses or answers that are obvious.

Don't be afraid of silence during a discussion. It often yields especially thoughtful comments.

Test questions before using them by attempting to answer them yourself.

When leading a discussion, pay attention to the mood of your group by "listening" with your eyes as well as your ears.

Guidelines for the Group

IMMERSION is designed to promote full engagement with the Bible for the purpose of growing faith and building up Christian community. While much can be gained from individual reading, a group Bible study offers an ideal setting in which to achieve these aims. Encourage participants to bring their Bibles and read from Scripture during the session. Invite participants to consider the following guidelines as they participate in the group:

Respect differences of interpretation and understanding.

Support one another with Christian kindness, compassion, and courtesy.

Listen to others with the goal of understanding rather than agreeing or disagreeing.

Celebrate the opportunity to grow in faith through Bible study.

Approach the Bible as a dialogue partner, open to the possibility of being challenged or changed by God's Word.

Recognize that each person brings unique and valuable life experiences to the group and is an important part of the community.

Reflect theologically—that is, be attentive to three basic questions: What does this say about God? What does this say about me/us? What does this say about the relationship between God and me/us?

Commit to a lived faith response in light of insights you gain from the Bible. In other words, what changes in attitudes (how you believe) or actions (how you behave) are called for by God's Word?

Group Sessions

The group sessions, like the chapters themselves, are built around three sections: "Claim Your Story," "Enter the Bible Story," and "Live the Story." Sessions are designed to move participants from an awareness of their own life story, issues, needs, and experiences into an encounter and dialogue with the story of Scripture and to make decisions integrating their personal stories and the Bible's story.

The session plans in the following pages will provide questions and activities to help your group focus on the particular content of each chapter. In addition to questions and activities, the plans will include chapter title, Scripture, and faith focus.

Here are things to keep in mind for all the sessions:

Prepare Ahead

Study the Scripture, comparing different translations and perhaps a paraphrase.

Read the chapter, and consider what it says about your life and the Scripture.

Gather materials such as large sheets of paper or a markerboard with markers.

Prepare the learning area. Write the faith focus for all to see.

Welcome Participants

Invite participants to greet one another.

Tell them to find one or two people and talk about the faith focus.

Ask: What words stand out for you? Why?

Guide the Session

Look together at "Claim Your Story." Ask participants to give their reactions to the stories and examples given in each chapter. Use questions from the session plan to elicit comments based on personal experiences and insights.

Ask participants to open their Bibles and "Enter the Bible Story." For each portion of Scripture, use questions from the session plan to help participants gain insight into the text and relate it to issues in their own lives.

Step through the activity or questions posed in "Live the Story." Encourage participants to embrace what they have learned and to apply it in their daily lives.

Invite participants to offer their responses or insights about the boxed material in "Across the Testaments," "About the Scripture," and "About the Christian Faith."

Close the Session
Encourage participants to read the following week's Scripture and chapter before the next session.

Offer a closing prayer.

1. Practical Wisdom
James 1:1–2:26

Faith Focus
Faith first gives blessings to the believer, then requires gracious response in kind.

Before the Session
Read the entire Book of James in preparation for the first two sessions of this study. On a large sheet of paper, print the following: What rules do you follow—at home, in the workplace, in your daily interactions?

Claim Your Story
As participants arrive, invite them to respond in writing to the questions you posed about rules. In the total group, invite persons to share a response to the first question posed in the study. Have they yielded to the temptation to blame someone else for their actions, and if so, who did they blame? A sibling? A friend? A colleague or boss? God? How would they define honesty and integrity?

Enter the Bible Story
Invite participants to indicate by a show of hands with which of the following statements they most agree:
- Salvation is a matter of grace working through faith. What I believe is very important.
- Salvation is about practicing what I preach following the teachings of Jesus.

Ask volunteers to share why they chose to respond as they did.

Note for the group that Martin Luther called this book an epistle of straw. How do participants respond to that?

Ask participants to find the first chapter of one of the following epistles: Romans, First Corinthians, Second Corinthians, Galatians, Ephesians, Philippians, or Colossians. Invite volunteers to read aloud the first few verses of each epistle. Then ask someone to read aloud James 1:1. What typical features of an epistle are lacking in James?

While some scholars have speculated that James may be a collection of essays, it may make more sense to view it as poetry. Ask a volunteer to review the characteristics of Hebrew poetry as described in the section of the study material titled "James's Poetic Prologue." Ask someone to read aloud the verses from Proverbs included in this section. Then ask someone to read verses 1:5b-8 of James as formatted in poetic form on page 13, as well as verses 13-15. What is the writer of James saying about wisdom? About those who do not participate in wisdom?

Ask volunteers to summarize the information in the sidebar about the Rule of Benedict. Does the group think there are parallels we might draw between the time of Benedict, when Christianity had become identified with the Roman Empire, and our contemporary context? Is it possible that Christians today might need ways to separate ourselves from our culture?

The study writer suggests that we may want to read the Book of James as a rule of life describing those practices that lead to a healthy, vibrant Christian life. Review with the group the rules they posted that guide their lives at home, in the workplace, and as they interact with others. Are some of the rules they noted ones that might make up a rule of Christian life?

Ask someone to read aloud James 2:14-26.Call attention to the study writer's definition of Christian practices. Note that they are called practices for a reason; we are intended to practice them over and over as a part of our Christian discipleship. Distribute paper and pens or pencils, and ask participants to take a few minutes to make two lists that answer these questions posed by the study writer: What are the things I do habitually that bring me closer to the way that Jesus lived? What are those practices that lead me farther away from the example Jesus set for us? After a few minutes, ask participants to pair up and share their lists. In the total group, ask each pair to share one practice from each list.

Live the Story

When, in participants' experience, has favoritism led to bad results, or even to tragedy? Note that this must have been a problem in the early Christian community. Invite a member of the group to read aloud 1 Corinthians 11:17-22, 27-34. Then ask: What was Paul's objection to the way the rich and the poor were treated when Christians gathered to celebrate the Lord's Supper? How do we and our congregation promote or resist showing favoritism toward those who are already privileged? Are there practices or ways of doing things in our community of faith that implicitly exclude those who are less privileged, whether because of access to wealth or to power?

Because prayer is one of the Christian practices that can be the most powerfully formative, join in a time of silent prayer, asking God to open participants to discernment about how they might move ever closer to the way that Jesus lived. Then invite them to name blessings they have received, giving thanks to God for those things. Encourage participants to consider how they are called to respond.

2. Worldly Values and Wisdom From Above
James 3:1–5:20

Faith Focus
Life in Christ forms us into a community that encourages us to put flesh on our words of faith by treating everyone impartially, speaking wisely, and showing compassion and generosity.

Before the Session
On a large sheet of paper, print the following: "Sticks and stones may break my bones, but names . . ." and get large, colored self-stick notes and pens or pencils for each participant. Gather magazines with advertising, newspaper ad sections, or ads from the Internet—enough for every two participants. On six separate large sheets of paper, print each of the elements of the rule of life from James as listed by the study writer and post them at intervals around your learning space. Get six felt-tipped markers.

Claim Your Story
Invite someone to summarize the story about the rabbi and the gossip. Then ask participants to share how they completed the aphorism you posted. Is it true that words can never hurt you, or can they be destructive? Discuss how social networking media like Twitter, Facebook, and e-mail can be an extension of the tongue. Ask volunteers to share a time when they would have liked to have snatched back hasty words or when they hit "send" or "reply all" on an imprudent message in the heat of the moment. How did they deal with the fallout? Did they attempt to make amends?

Enter the Bible Story
James places special responsibility on teachers to heed carefully the power of their words. Discuss who else might be placed in this category. How do participants deal with the heated rhetoric and partial truths in every political campaign? Is it possible to challenge how language is used?

Ask volunteers to name the three similes the writer of James uses to expand our understanding of the power of words (words are like a horse, like a ship, like a small flame that ignites a forest). List these on a large sheet of paper. Distribute pens or pencils and self-stick notes to the group. Challenge them to come up with their own similes from their contemporary context, and give them a few minutes to print their simile on a self-stick note. Then invite participants to attach their simile to the sheet and explain it to the group. Call the group's attention to verse 10, where James notes that blessing and cursing come from the same mouth, although this should not be so. How do Christians deal with issues (political, theological, or ethical) where they have widely divergent views? What steps can we take to discuss our differences in love without vilifying those whose opinions differ?

Ask someone to read aloud James 3:13-18. How would the group describe the wisdom from above? The study writer notes that James's intention is to describe what life might be like for communities torn apart by strife and favoritism for the wealthy if they followed his rule of life.

Ask group members to pair up and distribute the ads you brought. Call attention to the second paragraph of the study under the head "The High and the Mighty," and ask someone to read that paragraph aloud. Then ask participants to examine the ads to see what values are being expressed. What is the purpose of the ads (beyond simply to get you to buy the product)? How much is "enough"? What are the implications of the increasing gap between rich and poor in this country?

Would participants agree that while wealth is not evil in and of itself, it presents a danger to those who desire to live in God's ways? In what ways?

Live the Story

Call participants' attention to what the study writer summarizes as the rule of life presented in the Book of James and point out the posted sheets of paper with the six aspects of the rule. Divide the group into six pairs or small groups, or if your group is small, assign aspects to individual participants. Ask them to read over the rule and discuss the following briefly in their pair or group: What implications does this aspect of the rule have for others? How and about what are we called to confess our shortcomings around this aspect? Ask them to jot down what they discussed on the sheet of paper.

Remind participants that the study writer notes that, for James, the antidote to the dangers of this world includes prayer for others and the confession of our sins. Join together in a time of prayer, inviting each pair or small group to read their assigned aspect and then offer a sentence prayer incorporating their discussion. Challenge participants in the coming week to focus their prayers on the rule of life.

3. A Life of Grateful Obedience
1 Peter 1:1–2:12

Faith Focus

As Christians we are invited to seek holiness of life through grateful, joyful obedience.

Before the Session

If you have not already done so, read the entire Book of First Peter. In the center of a large sheet of paper, print the word "obedience." Prepare individual construction paper strips (at least one for each person) on which you print the linked images the study writer notes (stone-temple-race-priesthood-nation-people), one per strip. You will need some glue or tape. Every six strips will form one construction paper chain.

Claim Your Story

Invite participants to brainstorm around the word *obedience*. Remind them of the ground rules of brainstorming: They are to call out any response that comes to mind in the manner of free-form response. Responses are not to be critiqued. As responses are called out, print them around the central word on the large sheet of paper. When everyone has responded, invite persons to share any personal experiences they have had concerning obedience. Were participants' experiences largely positive or negative? Were group members taught, as was the study writer, to express gratitude at the same time they were taught obedience?

In First Peter, obedience and gratitude go hand in hand. What difference would it make if we approach life with an attitude of gratitude?

Enter the Bible Story

Call the group's attention to the phrase from the United Methodist prayer of confession, "free us for joyful obedience." Refer to the brainstorming list the group made. Which of the responses would be consistent with a joyful approach to life? Do any of the free association responses seem to indicate a reluctance to give up one's individualism? In our culture, we seem to have come to believe that to be truly joyful we have to be free to do whatever we want. How does the group respond to that? Discuss the difference the study writer notes between joy and happiness. What is the role of prayer in enabling us to rejoice regardless of our life circumstances?

The word *holy* means to be set apart for the purposes of God. This meaning helps us to appreciate the situation of those who would have originally heard this letter. Refer the group to the sidebar where the writer describes the original audience for First Peter (page 29). In what ways do the words *stranger* or *exile* apply to these people? Within our own cultural context, do these words apply to those of us who are Christian? Should they? How do we see ourselves as holy—set apart for God's purposes?

On a markerboard or a large sheet of paper, print the words "stone-temple-race-priesthood-nation-people." Explain that these six are linked images that describe what joyful hope and grateful obedience look like. Distribute to each person a strip of paper with one of the images written on it. Ask each participant to read over the information in the study about the assigned image. After a few minutes, ask participants to form small groups of six, with each group including all six images. Beginning with the image of stone, ask participants to briefly explain their image in turn, linking each strip to the next as one would make a paper chain and taping or gluing the link into the chain. Encourage them to not only explain their image but to also explain how it is linked to and deepens the previous image. At the conclusion of the small group discussion, each group should have a paper chain that visually illustrates the linked images.

Although these images have sometimes been perceived as excluding some people, the study writer sees them as expansive and inclusive. The only way to be excluded is not to choose to be a part of God's people. Is this view consistent with what we understand about what it means to be Christian? How can we be a part of bringing God's shalom to fruition for the world?

Ask a volunteer to read aloud the study writer's poem "From Dead Dry Rocks."

Live the Story

Suggest that participants choose one or more of the practices described on pages 34 and 35 that might help them live lives of joyful obedience and in which they can engage over the next week.

Expand on the idea of thinking back over the day and noting blessings by engaging in the practice of examination of conscience. Invite the group to sit quietly with their eyes closed, inviting God's presence in this moment. Then invite them to bring into consciousness those things for which they are grateful, naming each one and thanking God for them. Follow this with a time of bringing into consciousness those things for which they need forgiveness, and ask God's forgiveness. End by asking God's Spirit to reveal how the gifts you have been given are to be used.

4. Suffering Love
1 Peter 2:13–5:14

Faith Focus
Christians can embrace a life of suffering love because we know that suffering is not the final word. Love is.

Before the Session
Reflect on times when you have suffered, perhaps from unjust accusations or when you have been punished when you did not deserve it. What was your response? Were you left with feelings of anger, resentment, or the need to exact vengeance? How is it possible to transform experiences of suffering in ways that are meaningful?

Claim Your Story
Ask participants to name times when they were accused of something they didn't do and then punished unjustly for it. How did they feel about what happened? Ask them to name examples they have heard of where other persons suffered without deserving it. How are we as Christians to respond when we see others suffering through no fault of their own?

Enter the Bible Story
The writer of First Peter is concerned that Jesus' followers set themselves apart from the culture while at the same time living in harmony with their non-believing neighbors and with the structures of power. The study writer notes that many of them may have been immigrants or guest workers. In what ways are today's immigrants and guest workers set apart from our mainstream culture? What factors come into play if they are also part of another faith system, such as Islam or Buddhism? Is it possible that these "strangers" are vulnerable to being punished for crimes they do not commit? Do you know of any examples of times when Christians in our country today have experienced punishment for doing good?

In addressing the verses about submission to authority, the writer notes that it is dangerous to lift a text from the ancient world and apply it to contemporary life without examining the context to which it originally spoke. The writer of First Peter seems to be encouraging the followers of Jesus to avoid even the appearance of being lawbreakers. In the light of our world today, what are we to make of what the study writer calls a subversive statement, "Do this as God's slaves, and yet also as free people"? How might this apply to acts of civil disobedience, such as those during the Civil Rights Movement or the Occupy Wall Street Movement more recently? Is it possible to respect the institutions of government while still being involved in such actions? How do Christians balance respect for the law with their ultimate loyalty to God?

Divide the group into two smaller groups. Ask one group to read 1 Peter 2:18-25 and the portions of the study that relate to slaves and submission, and the other to read 1 Peter 3:1-9 and the portions of the study dealing with spouses and submission. Ask each group to consider both the texts themselves, their original context, and the arguments made in the study. What do we make of what the text is saying about submission? How does the text speak to our context today? Are you persuaded by the arguments of the study writer that human suffering must be put in the context of Christ's suffering? What would you say to those who would use these texts to justify the subordinate role of wives, the institution of slavery, or the subordination of one racial group to another?

When groups have had time to discuss, challenge them to report on their discussion to the total group. Look together at the twentieth-century example from Viktor Frankl's book *Man's Search for Meaning*. Does the group agree that it is possible to find meaning even in extreme suffering?

Ask volunteers to name the two signs that indicate that those who suffer are finished with sin. Jesus' example transforms suffering from a mark of shame into a badge of honor. Does the group agree or disagree that Christians should not expect the world to accommodate us, but rather should expect to be mocked because of Christ's name?

Live the Story

Invite participants to respond to the following scenario:

You live a quiet life in a rural area. One day an armed gunman forces his way into the school your children attend, lines up the children and their teachers, and opens fire, killing several of the children, including your own, before killing himself.

What does the group think their thoughts and actions might be? What if the gunman had been captured instead of committing suicide? This scenario is very similar to a real-life tragedy in an Amish community in recent years when that community reached out to the family of the perpetrator with love and forgiveness. Discuss the final two questions the study writer poses.

Close by reading the final blessing of the letter (1 Peter 5:10-11).

5. Awaiting the End of the World
2 Peter 1:1–3:18

Faith Focus

As we wait for the day of the Lord, we live as Jesus taught, unswayed by false teachers and disinterested in the length of the wait.

Before the Session

Prepare two posters with the following text: (1) Save the Date! Return of Christ, May 21, 2011 (wecanknow.com). (2) That was awkward. "No one knows the day or the hour . . ." Matthew 24:36.

Check with your pastor to find out if your congregation has formulated a vision and a mission statement. If so, make copies for participants, or print them on a large sheet of paper. If you do not have such a statement, print "God's vision for our congregation . . ." and "Our Mission . . ." on a large sheet of paper.

Claim Your Story

Invite the group to reflect on the following: To whom do I offer my deepest loyalty? To what loyalty do my actions point? Do I appear to give my ultimate allegiance to a charismatic preacher? A political party? My nation? My career? If I asked those closest to me, what would they say about where my loyalties lie?

Enter the Bible Story

Ask participants what they believe about the end time. Are they concerned about when the end of the world will come, or are they pretty much indifferent to the speculation that arises from time to time?

Point out the two posters. Remind participants of the flurry of news coverage in the spring of 2011 over yet another prediction of the exact date the world would come to an end—this one announced around the world on billboards like poster #1. When May 21, 2011, came and went and the world continued on as usual, another billboard with the message of poster #2 appeared on many social networking sites.

The study writer observes that we are to spend our time, however much there may be, in life-giving activities rather than in the life-destroying behavior that false teachers promote. Invite someone to read aloud 2 Peter 1:5-7. If we knew for sure that the world would be coming to an end in a week, how would we spend that time? Would we choose to do those things that would reflect what these verses are talking about?

In our time, there are many false prophets, not only at the head of religious cults like the one in Guyana but in the secular realm as well. Invite participants to name persons or corporate entities that they consider to promote life-destroying behaviors. Call the group's attention to the sidebar, "Four Kinds of Monks." Who are contemporary *sarabaites* who want to live by their rules and no other, or *gyrovagues* who only seem to want to exploit others rather than building up community?

The following statements summarize three divergent positions on the Second Coming:

- Scripture provides a roadmap with clues that can tell exactly when the Second Coming will occur. Many of the events we are experiencing now point to the end time.
- The Second Coming is an ancient artifact. The world may end because of human folly, but not with a Second Coming of Christ.
- We can't know for sure when the Second Coming will be. We must trust in God and continue God's work until that time.

How does the group respond to the idea that the delay in the Second Coming is not through God's neglect or forgetfulness, but because God desires as many people as possible to respond to God's invitation in Jesus Christ to be a part of God's dream for creation? Second Peter was encouragement to communities trying to live faithfully in the midst of persecution and oppression. What are the impediments to faithful living for us today?

Live the Story

If your congregation has vision and mission statements, distribute copies or post the sheet of paper. Invite someone to read them aloud. Emphasize that these statements are the result of a process of discerning what God is calling us to do as a faith community, an attempt to define in words what our job is as followers of Jesus as we wait for the day of the Lord.

If your congregation has not yet formulated such statements, invite participants to be in prayer for discernment about what they might be. They may want to talk with your pastor about initiating a process of discernment.

Reflect together in silence on the following: What is my vocation? How is God calling me to participate in working for shalom? How is my vocation a part of the larger calling of this congregation? Close by praying that God's Spirit will guide participants in exploring this at a deeper level.

6. Living in the Light
1 John 1:1–3:24

Faith Focus
God's light shining through us in loving actions toward others identifies us as followers of Jesus.

Before the Session
Read the entire book of First John in preparation for this session and the next. If your church has stained-glass windows, walk through your sanctuary, focusing on each window and the figures it depicts. If these figures are of persons, how was the light of God reflected in each person's life? On a large sheet of paper, print the following question: What would happen if we in our church pledged to look for ways to reflect God's light and love by the good we do for others who are less fortunate?

Obtain a traditional pillar candle or one of the newer flameless LED battery candles.

Claim Your Story
Invite participants to reflect on those persons they would identify as people through whom the light shines. In what ways did each of these people reflect God's light in their lives? Ask each person to reflect in silence on areas of their own lives where the light of God shines with strength and other areas where they do not reflect that light as clearly.

Enter the Bible Story
Encourage the group to listen for the action words in the opening verses of First John (on page 56) as a volunteer reads them aloud.

How do participants respond when they have committed a sin—by asking forgiveness or with denial? Often denial takes the form of elaborate rationalizations. Invite someone to read aloud 1 John 1:8-10, familiar words often used following the corporate prayer of confession. The first step in acknowledging our sin is the recognition that we are not the source of the light. Rather we are to live in such a way that we reflect God's light. How do we do that?

Ask participants to share any experiences when there was no artificial light source. What was it like to experience near or total darkness? What activities were made more difficult or even impossible?

What is the one true test that will show that the new/old commandment First John is talking about is being followed? Ask participants to reflect on times when they may have harbored ill-will or even hatred for someone. In what ways did they experience blindness? When did they stumble? If we are grounded in Jesus, we are enabled to make loving choices. This relationship with Jesus is not initiated by us, but by God.

On a large sheet of paper, print the following: "light/darkness; righteousness/sin; love/hate; life/death." What is the relationship between these paired concepts? What allows us to move from the negative side of each equation to the positive side? Invite the group to consider what Christian practices they engage in that feed a dynamic, growing relationship with Jesus.

Call the group's attention to the following statement by the study writer: "After all, love is not just a feeling; it is a way of living, of treating others." Ask the group to respond to the assertion that if we have material possessions and ignore another person's need, then the love of God is not in us. Ask participants to comment on how they think one should respond to persons in the following circumstances: a family with children, living on welfare; a single parent with children, working two low-wage jobs; an alcoholic living on the streets; a formerly incarcerated person who is unable to find a job. What helps us determine how to respond? How does self-condemnation get in the way of our love for our brothers and sisters? In the experience of participants, what else can get in the way? What can motivate us to move beyond talking about love in an adult study class to active participation in God's loving work in the world?

Live the Story
Ask participants to pair up and discuss briefly the posted question. Then under that question, print the following: What would happen if we in our church pledged to reflect God's light and love by reaching out to others as beloved children, our brothers and sisters? Ask participants to discuss this question with their partner. Invite observations about the two questions. Does reframing "those less fortunate" as "our brothers and sisters" transform how we might relate to one another?

Invite the group to form a circle and place the lighted pillar candle in the center of the circle, turning off the lights and closing shades to darken the room. Ask participants to focus their sight, not on the candle, but on the face of each person in turn. Reflect on how God's light is reflected in the lives of these persons and silently pray that they may participate actively in reflecting God's light in the world.

7. Love Is a Policy
1 John 4:1–3 John 15

Faith Focus
For followers of Jesus, self-giving, extravagant love for everyone is a deliberate choice, independent of circumstances.

Before the Session
On a large sheet of paper, prepare a Venn diagram—three large linked circles. There should be an overlap where each circle intersects with a second, with one section in the center where all three overlap. Label the circles First John, Second John, and Third John. Cut three large hearts from red construction paper. Label one *érōs*, one *philía*, and one *agápē*.

Claim Your Story
Invite the group to respond to this question: Have you ever observed or been a part of a situation in which Christian love overcame hatred? What made that possible? Ask participants to respond to this open-ended prompt in the light of their discussion: If it weren't for Jesus, I would . . ."

Enter the Bible Story
First John reveals that God's Spirit has been given to the readers of the letter, with the caveat that not every spirit comes from God. Ask participants to cite examples in their own experience or about which they have read or heard where a group or an individual professed to be Christian and yet acted in ways that are counter to God's love. Central to First John is the understanding that Jesus is human as well as divine. To confess that Jesus Christ has become human is to act as if God's love has indeed been born and walks among us, and then to follow that example. Love is the primary and most profound witness to faith in God. What does it mean that we abide in God and God abides in us?

Ask someone to summarize what the study writer has to say about John Wesley's idea that people could be made perfect in love. Who takes the initiative in this perfecting?

Divide the group into three smaller groups or pairs. Give each small group one of the paper hearts and invite them to read the information in the sidebar on page 68 explaining their assigned type of love, jotting down information on the heart. Are there types of love that are primarily emotion? If *agápē* is the kind of love we experience from God and strive to show to the world, how is emotion involved? Is it possible to show agápē love to a person we don't like, or whom we may distrust or even fear?

The study writer calls Second and Third John reminder notes of some of the issues raised in First John. Call the group's attention to the Venn diagram of three intersecting circles, and tell them that they will use these circles to compare and contrast the three books. First ask participants to name ways each book is unique, and record these in the areas of each circle that do not overlap another circle. Then look at ways Second and Third John are alike that distinguish them from First John, and record these in the areas where those two circles overlap. Finally record ways all three books are alike in the center section where all three circles overlap. Are there any characteristics that First John shares with Second John, or that First John shares with Third John?

Although epistles were meant to be read aloud to communities, this is a poor substitute for face-to-face communication. What about in the ways we show God's love to others, particularly those who are very different from us? How is a relationship altered when we are able to interact face-to-face?

Live the Story

Remind the group of the three types of love they discussed. Note that while Greek includes three words for love, English only has one. However, the word *love* is used to describe a whole range of different experiences, as the study writer explains. Invite the group to respond, popcorn style, to the prompt "I love . . . ," calling out anything that comes to mind. List these on a large sheet of paper. Invite participants to comment on the range and nuance of meanings we assign to the concept. What does the word *love* convey in our culture?

The study writer reports on a conversation with a professor who noted that love is not a feeling, love is a policy. John's letters emphasize that love—*agápē*— is our policy because it is God's policy. Invite the group to reflect on the three questions that close this session: What are you doing to implement love as a policy? What more could you be doing? What more are you ready to do? Join together in a prayer that God's Spirit will lead you to discern the answers to these questions and to act on them.

8. Holding Fast to What Is Important
Jude

Faith Focus
Earnestly embracing a life that reflects God's grace and love defeats all the efforts of false teachers.

Before the Session
Head a large sheet of paper with the words, "Lost in a Dense Forest." Cut strips of brown construction paper and provide pens or pencils and tape. On another sheet, print the following: "I'll do whatever I want. It's a free country. It's nobody else's business." Read the narratives about Balaam (Numbers 16) and Korah (Numbers 22:22-40) and be prepared to summarize these less-than-familiar stories for the group. If you like, download a clip from YouTube or get a CD of the movie soundtrack of the song "Tradition" from *Fiddler on the Roof* for the closing and make arrangements to play it. Reflect on what traditions have been formative for you.

Claim Your Story
As participants arrive, invite them to silently read the first two paragraphs of Chapter 8 and to reflect on what issues populate their own personal forest. On strips of brown paper, they can record what their forest is, and then tape their strips to the sheet to represent trees. Discuss things that may distract us from what will ultimately be the true path out of the forest we inhabit and in which we may be lost.

Enter the Bible Story
The godless people to whom Jude is referring are most likely traveling evangelists who preach that freedom in Jesus Christ releases us from all moral constraints. Call the group's attention to the posted sheet. Does the group agree with the study writer that this is probably the most common interpretation of freedom in our culture today, or would they express it some other way? Is this interpretation destructive to Christian faith and life and if so, how? As Christians, how would we define freedom? The study writer contrasts favoritism, doing good only for those who can do us some good, with promoting the common good, addressing the needs of the vulnerable for the good of all. Which attitude seems to have gained ascendancy today? What are some implications?

On a markerboard, print the word "antinomianism," and invite a volunteer to define it. Ask participants to silently read Acts 15:1-21 to refresh their memories about the debate about following the law that was affecting the church to whom Jude addressed this letter. Then have someone read aloud the two passages from Galatians on page 75. Does the church today have similar debates around a rigid adherence to some doctrinal standards? How does it play itself out in our denominational structures? In our local churches?

Invite volunteers to briefly summarize the stories of the Exodus (Exodus 14), the destruction of Sodom and Gomorrah (Genesis 19:1-29), and Cain's murder of Abel (Genesis 4:1-16), as well as the two stories in the sidebar (page 76) from apocryphal writings. Because fewer persons are probably familiar with the references to Balaam and Korah, summarize them for the group yourself. What are images of faithlessness and the resulting punishment in each of these stories?

Review together the metaphor the writer of Jude employs to describe people whose concern is only for their own welfare. As participants name them, list them on a markerboard. Then challenge participants to think about persons or groups in our culture today who show the same lack of concern for others. Give them a few minutes to think of metaphors that describe these self-centered ones, then invite them to name the metaphors, and list these along with those from Jude.

Ask someone to read aloud verses 17-23, asking that participants listen for the verbs in these verses. Invite the group to name the three categories into which the study writer categorizes this passage. Although we in our churches are certainly not under siege in the same way as Jude's audience, we are experiencing our own conflicts and pressures from a secularized culture. Are Jude's instructions a good basic outline for us about living in community today? Are there any other suggestions we would add? Ask someone to read aloud the study writer's poem, based on these verses (page 77).

Live the Story

If you choose, play or (or show the video clip) of the song "Tradition" from *Fiddler on the Roof.* Traditions are not only important, they are formative. Invite the group to respond to the questions posed on page 79 about traditions that have shaped them in life-enhancing ways. How do we strengthen and expand those traditions that form us in positive ways? Are there any traditions that do not contribute to our growth as disciples? If so, how do we let go of those or transform them?

Close by reading the blessing that ends the Book of Jude.